Quickscript

By Adele Booth Blanchard

Arco Publishing, Inc.
New York

Published by Arco Publishing, Inc.
215 Park Avenue South, New York, N.Y. 10003

Library of Congress Cataloging in Publication Data

Blanchard, Adele Booth.
Quickscript : the fast and simple shorthand method.

Includes index.
1. Shorthand—Quickscript. I. Title.
Z56.2.S6B55 653′.2 82-6703
ISBN 0-668-05572-3 AACR2

Printed in the United States of America

10 9 8 7 6 5 4 3 2 1

To
M. W. M. G.
and
R. G. B.

sine qua non

TABLE OF CONTENTS

INTRODUCTION

Who can benefit from learning Quickscript? Anyone who takes notes for any reason: journalists, executives and secretaries, administrators and students.

The advantages of Quickscript are twofold. Since it is based upon ordinary script writing, it may be learned more easily and quickly than any symbolic method; it is also much easier to read and transcribe even after the passage of considerable time. The few symbols it employs are written in a way which follows the normal flow of standard penmanship; because Quickscript resembles regular penmanship so closely, what you learn can be incorporated naturally in everyday writing.

This system has been successfully taught for over twenty-five years and its utility has been thoroughly tested.

For those who wish to be fluent in taking notes, the mastery of the first seven lessons and the sounds of the next five lessons will provide a good foundation. You can then select from the remaining lessons whatever will best fit the special vocabulary of your business or study. The content of each lesson can be used immediately to improve notetaking skills.

To take dictation, you will need to know the complete course so thoroughly that you have no hesitation in remembering what you have learned. Your progress will be in proportion to your study and practice.

The shorthand is presented so that it can be self-taught. A useful tool for teaching yourself is a tape recorder, particularly if your goal is to take dictation.

The text is divided into nineteen lessons which teach the sounds, theory, prefixes, suffixes, and memory words comprising the system. Material concerning these topics is presented within each lesson in the same order and under separate headings. The individual items under each heading are numbered consecutively within that category. Each lesson also includes a vocabulary list, a phrase drill, and practice sentences which provide a review of what has been learned up to that point.

Immediately after each lesson, practice guidelines are given which are cross-referenced to the appropriate section title and item number of the preceding lesson. The guidelines amplify the lesson and give hints on how to write the material presented in it. Speed building paragraphs are included after every fourth lesson.

The twentieth lesson covers business correspondence with special abbreviations to be used only in writing the address, salutation, and the complimentary close of letters. Six business letters comprise the practice part of this lesson.

The last lesson in the text is devoted entirely to building speed. It is based on the most frequently used words in the business vocabulary. Five groups of sentences concentrate on the 300 most frequently used words, the 600 most frequently used, and so on. Practice letters follow. An additional feature of this lesson is a section of speed tests that have been used by businesses to test the shorthand skills of secretarial applicants.

The text concludes with an index of memory words and memory phrases.

Special thanks are due to Eleaner Ferrell Gyory for her suggestions and assistance.

The cooperation of Ames Agency, Helen Edwards and Staff, Eric Short, and Thomas Temporaries for permission to use materials included in the last lesson is appreciated.

GUIDELINES FOR USE OF TEXT

Quickscript is exceptionally easy to understand. Learning any shorthand, however, takes active participation. It is not enough to read and understand each lesson—you must have a stenographic notebook available and a pen in your hand and start at once to write what you are learning. Frequently check your efforts against the examples in the text. Be particular about how you form your letters, and remember that the larger you write, the longer it takes.

Although much of the lesson material is so simple that there seems to be no need for additional comment, always refer to the Practice Guidelines which follow each lesson. The cross-referencing by section titles (Sounds, Theory, etc.) and by numbers under each section makes this easy.

When you come to the Vocabulary, the Phrase Drills, and the Lesson Review sentences, practice reading the shorthand before you practice writing. Cover the transcription of the shorthand with a paper and read the shorthand lists and sentences several times; check to see whether your reading is correct. Then cover the shorthand and start writing. When you have checked and know you are writing correctly, drill as suggested in the Practice Guidelines. If you own a tape recorder, it will be helpful to record the material you want to practice and let the tape dictate to you.

Practicing the Lesson Review sentences will build speed, but they are not designed to test speed. Their primary purpose is to teach the application of the shorthand sounds and rules given in the lessons they conclude. The Speed Building sections which are inserted after every four lessons will give you an opportunity to develop and test your speed.

LESSON I

Quickscript is based on the letters of the alphabet; therefore it is important to use good standard penmanship. The accepted forms of the letters of the alphabet which the shorthand uses are as follows:

a b c d e (do not use ε) f g h i j l n
o p q r s (do not use S) t u v x y z

See Practice Guidelines for Lesson I and then write these letters in your notebook and check your penmanship (omit *k*, *m*, and *w*; do not dot *i* or *j*).

Only actual sounds are written: (k)*no*(w), (w)*rit*(e), (g)*na*(w), *ha*(t)*ch*, *thr*(o)*u*(gh). Write *only* what is heard. Never visualize words; *listen.*

Sounds

1. c = sound of *k* as in *kick* and *cat.* It is called *k.* The longhand *k* is never written to form words in Quickscript.
2. s = sound of *s* as in *seen* and *certain.* It is written as shown in the middle or at the end of a word. At the beginning of a word, it is written s and is called "initial *s.*" To form this letter, eliminate the upward stroke of a full *s*: s. Keep the letter size normal.
3. g = sound of *g* as in *gift.* It is called *guh.*
4. j = sound of *j* as in *judge* and *gem.*

5. *t* is written three ways: at the beginning of a word, "initial *t*" is *t* ; at the end of a word, "final *t*" is *t* ; neither of these is crossed. In the middle of a word, "medial *t*" is written as usual: *t* .

6. *q* = sound of *qw* as in *quick* and *sequel.*

Theory

1. Vowels are omitted between two consonants. The five vowels are *a*, *e*, *i*, *o*, and *u*.

lodge	*lj*	quick	*qc*	keep	*cp*
rough	*rf*	tell	*tl*	let	*lt*
cease	*ss*	happen	*hpn*	judge	*jj*
wrap	*rp*	civil	*svl*	college	*clj*

2. Pronounced vowels at the end of a word are written.

high	*hi*	say	*sa*	notify	*ntfi*
pay	*pa*	new	*nu*	follow	*flo*
fee	*fe*	value	*vlu*	relay	*rla*

3. A dot may indicate the sound of *i* in the body of a word.

via	*via*	kitten	*·ctn*	sign	*sin*	fit	*ft*

Memory Words

Memory Words are shortened forms of the most frequently used words. They do not follow the rules given in Theory.

1.	*u*	you, your	3.	*a*	at
2.	*)*	the	4.	*n*	in

5.	s	is, his	9.	v	have, very
6.	t	it	10.	e	he
7.	(n)	not	11.	+	and
8.	r	are, our, hour	12.	o	of

Vocabulary

In practicing, connect the letters that compose one word; do not lift your pen within a word.

1.	bc	back	13.	st	sought
2.	cd	could	14.	jb	job
3.	fl	file	15.	pc	pack
4.	fnl	final	16.	tl	tell
5.	no	know	17.	vlu	value
6.	bgn	begin	18.	se	see
7.	hi	high	19.	dpst	deposit
8.	dd	did	20.	jj	judge
9.	ys	yes	21.	nc	knock
10.	hf	half	22.	yt	yet
11.	gt	get	23.	sa	say
12.	qt	quit	24.	nts	notice

Phrases

In shorthand, a phrase is composed of several words which are easily written together. The purpose of phrasing is to increase the speed of writing and reading shorthand. Just as individual letters in longhand are immediately recognized as a word, so are phrased words in shorthand recognized as a thought unit.

1. / is usually joined to the word before it.

gv	give the	o	of the	v	have the
cp	keep the	tc	take the	r	are the

2. Pronouns are usually joined to verbs.

ur	you are	iv	I have	ts	it is
ecd	he could	udd	you did	ths	it has

3. Prepositional phrases are written together.

o	of the	nr	in our	os	of his
ar	at our	ot	of it	nu	in your

4. Phrase after conjunctions.

and he is &es   as you know asuno   so are sor

Phrase Drill

1.	ru	are you the	8.	s	is the
2.	&iv	and I have	9.	&vu	and have you
3.	e&i	he and I	10.	edsn	he does not
4.	&	and the	11.	ur	you are the
5.	rn	are not	12.	ts	it is the
6.	ibgn	I begin the	13.	ar	at our
7.	o	of the	14.	tsn	it is not the

Punctuation Marks

The following punctuation marks always start with the same stroke: from a little under the writing line, up and forward to it.

/	= period	^	= question mark
x	= paragraph	>	= comma

Only the paragraph requires a pen-lift. Other punctuation marks are as follows: hyphen = =, parentheses = ( ); write others as usual and circle them: (;) (:) (!) .

Lesson Review

Read the following shorthand; then check your efforts against the transcription in longhand which follows. Compare the difference in length between the two passages.

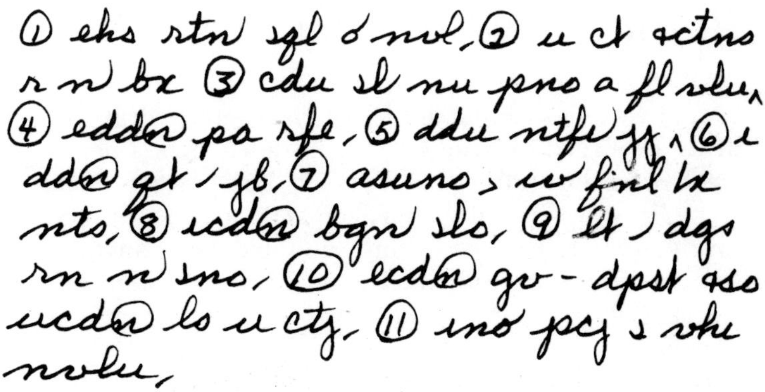

(1) He has written the sequel of the novel. (2) Your cat and kittens are in the box. (3) Could you sell the new piano at full value? (4) He did not pay our fee. (5) Did you notify the judge? (6) I did not quit the job. (7) As you know, I have the final tax notice. (8) I could not begin the solo. (9) Let the dogs run in the snow. (10) He could not give a deposit and so you could not lease your cottage. (11) I know the package is very high in value.

Practice Guidelines for Lesson I

Skill in writing shorthand is based on repetitive drill. Students are urged to write with a pen rather than a pencil, and to use stenographic notebooks in their practice. Fill as many lines (writing all the way across the page) as it takes for the script to become smooth and rapid. Since anything you write must be read, good standard penmanship is essential. Save your individual "style" of writing for social occasions.

Note that *a, c, d, g, o,* and *q* all start above the writing line: a c; not a c.

Sounds

2. To learn the correct form of "initial *s*," write a full *s*; then ignoring the first upward stroke, write over and over on the rest of the letter:  . Fill a few lines of your notebook with this letter. Be sure the downward stroke does not curl at the top: , not  .

5. Practice "initial *t*" the same way you practiced initial *s*:  ; write the full *t* and then ignoring the first upward stroke, write over and over on the downward stroke. Final *t*: The down stroke of *t* goes straight to the writing line and then retraces the stroke a short way up and ends to the right:  .

6.  must have the *qw* sound; therefore it cannot be written in *cute* or *culinary*; neither can it be written when a word ends in the spelling *que* as in *antique*.

In writing the six sounds of this lesson, say the sounds as you write. After you have filled a few lines for each letter individually, do the same thing in groups of three. Say "*k*, *s*, initial *s*" over and over, increasing your speed as your writing becomes smoother; "*guh*, *j*, initial *t*," etc. Check frequently with the text to be sure you are forming your letters correctly. Remember not to dot either  or .

Theory

Note that you do not lift your pen in the middle of a word.

3. The sound of *i* in the body of a word need not be in-

dicated, but often putting in the dot will speed transcription; in a few cases it will distinguish between words that are written the same way: fit *ft*, fat *ft*.

Vocabulary

Many words in the vocabulary lists have more than one meaning. For instance 2, *cd*, could also mean cad, kid, code, or cud. The passage in which the word occurs will clarify which meaning is correct.

Phrases

What and how much you phrase becomes a matter of judgment. The rules suggested here will begin to give you a feeling for phrasing. Phrasing too much is as bad as phrasing too little—speed in writing must be balanced by ease in reading. With experience you will sense which words group naturally for rapid writing and reading.

Dictate to Yourself as You Write

Drill with Theory examples, Memory Words, Phrases, and Vocabulary the same way you practiced Sounds. Your dictation should push you to writing more and more quickly. Use a tape recorder if you have one. Dictate all new material very slowly; then mix up the words and phrases, and gradually increase the speed. Check on your penmanship—can you read what you have written? Review the strokes that seem more difficult. You are establishing writing habits; with good habits you will never have any trouble reading your shorthand.

Lesson Review

Practice reading the shorthand before you practice writing it. Then referring only to the longhand, write these sentences in shorthand. Check your work. When you are sure you can write the sentences correctly, drill as suggested above. Keep your writing controlled and keep it small.

How to Make Corrections

Never try to erase or write over an incorrect or poorly written word: put a line through it and go on. 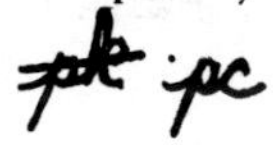

LESSON II

Sounds

1.  = sounds of *w* and *wh* as in *way* and *when*. It is an abbreviated form of *w*:  ; it starts above the writing line, follows the line the same length as a longhand *w* and ends above it. Check the Practice Guidelines to see how other letters are written with it.

2.  = *m*. It is an abbreviated form of *m*:  . It begins from the writing line, rises above it the height of an ordinary letter, and ends on the line; it is the same length as a longhand *m*. The Practice Guidelines illustrate how other letters are written with it.

3.  = sound of *ch* as in *chat*; it is called *chay*. Keep it small.

Now review these sounds as suggested in Practice Guidelines for Lesson I.

Memory Words

1.		a, an	5.		am, him
2.		be, but, been, by, buy	6.		for
3.		was	7.		to, two, too
4.		people, put, up	8.		can

9. upon
10. were, with
11. her, had
12. do, due, day, daily

Vocabulary

1.	will	13.	switch
2.	limit	14.	gallon
3.	some	15.	make
4.	what	16.	music
5.	model	17.	we
6.	college	18.	such
7.	which	19.	much
8.	gem	20.	check
9.	would	21.	one
10.	may	22.	have
11.	metal	23.	me
12.	lunch	24.	when

Phrases

1. Phrase infinitives.

   to get   to be   to pay

2. Phrase the parts of a verb together. Exception: 2 is not joined to the word before it.

   it will be   you have been

edlc we would like es zg he is to go

lamvb it may not have been

3. Phrase natural groups of words that can stand alone.

vl very well bnons by no means

Phrase Drill

1.	zvb	to have been	11.	nv	one of the
2.	so E	so much	12.	a E	at which
3.	ecd	he can do	13.	cdvb	could have been
4.	zc	to make	14.	bl	by mail
5.	dduv	did you have the	15.	nur	when you are
6.	lzsd	it was said	16.	zgvme	to give me
7.	ev	we are the	17.	hfdn	half done
8.	zdne	to deny	18.	hsnb	has not been
9.	amv	may not have	19.	vusn	have you seen
10.	ecnb	he cannot be	20.	u	with you

Contractions

An apostrophe signals a contraction.

v'n haven't z'n wasn't

Lesson Review

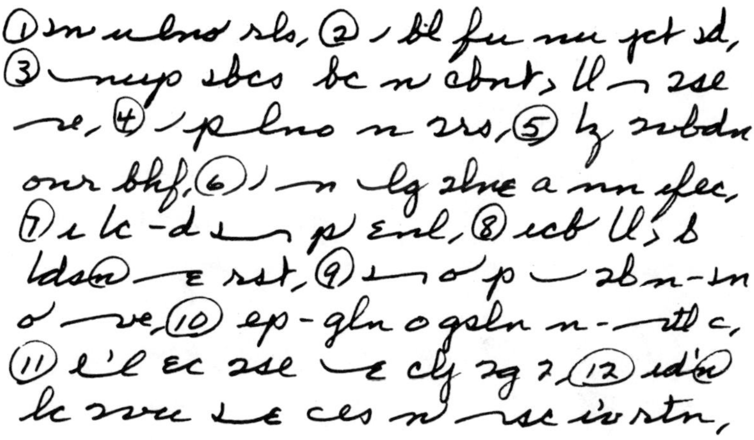

1. Soon you will know the rules. 2. The bill for your new jacket is due. 3. When you put his books back in the cabinet, tell him to see me. 4. The people will know in two hours. 5. It was to have been done on our behalf. 6. The man will go to lunch at noon if he can. 7. I take a daily swim up the channel. 8. I can buy the tool, but it does not match our set. 9. Some of the people were to be in a scene of the movie. 10. He put a gallon of gasoline in a metal can. 11. He'll check to see which college to go to. 12. I don't like to have you switch keys in the music I've written.

Practice Guidelines for Lesson II

Sounds

1. is used with other letters as follows

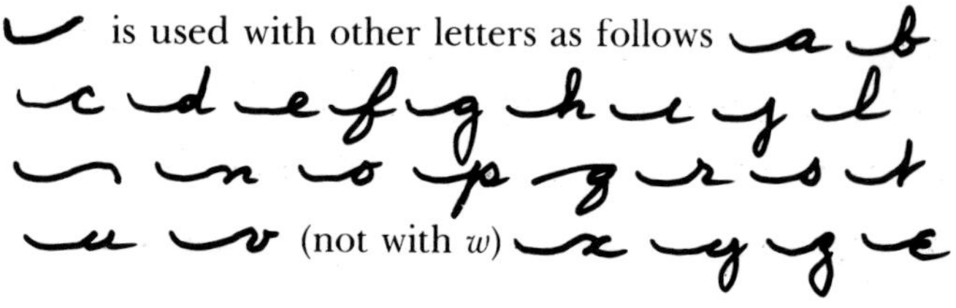

2. is used with other letters as follows:

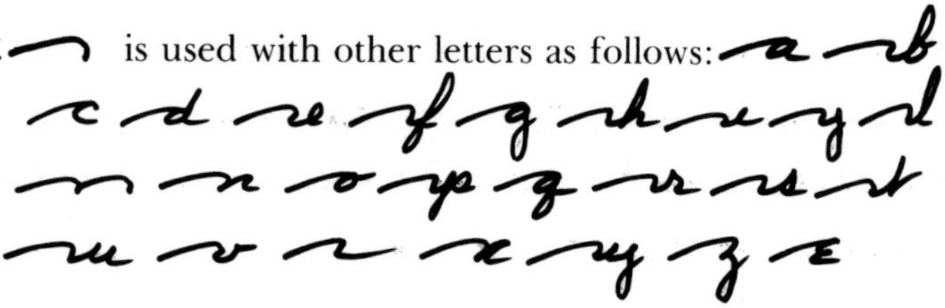

Note the similarity between and : the *r* must be formed properly to be read correctly. Also compare and and you will see why the full *y* must be written after the is completed.

3. should be no higher than other letters; a large means something else.

Phrase Drill

Just as some words in a list can be read several ways, so some phrases in a list can be read more than one way: 3, he could; 6, it was sad; 10, he cannot buy; 20, were you. As with the words, so with the phrases: within a sentence the correct reading becomes obvious.

Contractions

Contractions can also be written as you sound them: I'll = *i'l* or *i'l* ; he'll = *e'l* or *e'l* ; you'd = *u'd* or *u'd*

Lesson Review

After you can read the shorthand easily, work on the first sentence until you can write it readily before you go on to the next one.

LESSON III

Sounds

1. *f* = sound of *th*; it is called *ith*. The stroke above the writing line is like an *f*; the stroke below the writing line is like a *g*.

bf	both	ft	thought
sf	smooth	tf	tooth
pf	path	mfd	method
ff	thief	ff	faith
fc	thick	fs	thus
fn	thin	fss	thesis

2. s = sound of *st*; it is called "Cooper *s*." Keep it small.

sp	stop	bgs	biggest
ms	mist	los	lowest
ps	post	psn	piston
fs	fast	cs	coast
ws	west	jss	justice
sa	stay	sil	style

Theory

1. At the end of a word, *t* is omitted after a long vowel.

vo vote   ri right

da	date	bo	boat
—e	meet	‿e	wheat
rla	relate	pli	polite
su	suit	cu	cute

2. Accented initial vowels are usually written.

it—	item	unt	unit
eql	equal	if	if
opn	open	ast	asset

Note: When a word begins with a first syllable consisting of a short vowel plus *l*, *m*, *n*, or *x*, do not write the vowel.

njn	engine	nc—	income
lva	elevate	—fss	emphasis
xpdi	expedite	xjn	oxygen

3. Unaccented initial vowels are usually omitted.

bv	above	ln	alone
rv	arrive	nlss	analysis
rjnl	original	gp	equip

True Suffixes

A suffix is a word ending. A true suffix is an addition to an already complete word.

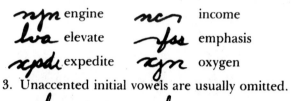

1. . = *-ed*:	raised	rs.	valued	vlu.
	delighted	dli.	checked	Ec.
2. l = *-ly*:	lovely	lvl	quickly	qcl
	rapidly	rpdl	locally	lcll

3. / = *-ing*: being; having; meeting; seeking

4. f = *-ful*: thoughtful; faithful; meaningful; restful

Memory Words

1. then, than
2. all
3. age
4. they
5. there, their
6. assistant, assistance
7. this
8. that
9. always
10. after, afternoon
11. note
12. ago, again, against

Vocabulary

1. youthful
2. eat
3. opening
4. restful
5. though
6. must
7. date
8. waited
9. system
10. assisting
11. exodus
12. come
13. receipt
14. faithful
15. theme
16. existed
17. past
18. elevate

19.	lgll	legally
20.	nvd.	invaded
21.	sel	sweetly
22.	qo´	quoting
23.	svc	civic
24.	pa	pay
25.	ad.	aided
26.	bs	best
27.	lf	wealth
28.	ht	hit
29.	be	beat
30.	bf	both
31.	qi	quite
32.	if	if

Phrase Drill

1.	iddno	I did not know
2.	lo-e	all of which
3.	fsn	this is not
4.	iffs	if this is the
5.	mvb	might have been
6.	vurd	have you read
7.	trhsb	there has been
8.	pnrse	upon receipt
9.	tyvb	they have been
10.	ervu	we wrote you
11.	uvh	you have had
12.	ulnt	you will note
13.	af	after the
14.	Lsb	it must be
15.	cun	can you not
16.	jsasl	just as well
17.	onfl	on file
18.	tm	to him
19.	fab	this may be
20.	scasf	such as this
21.	euc	which you can

Lesson Review

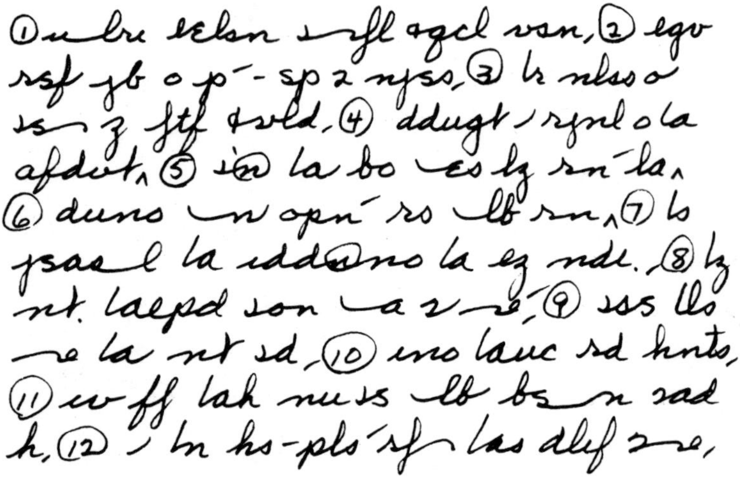

1. You will write each lesson smoothly and quickly very soon. 2. He gave our staff the job of putting a stop to injustice. 3. Their analysis of the system was thoughtful and valid. 4. Did you get the original of that affidavit? 5. Isn't that the boat which is always running late? 6. Do you know when the opening race will be run? 7. It is just as well that I did not know that he was indicted. 8. It was noted that he paid his own way to the meeting. 9. His assistant tells me that the note is due. 10. I know that you can read her notes. 11. I have faith that her new assistant will be the best one to aid her. 12. The tune has a pulsing rhythm that is delightful to me.

Practice Guidelines for Lesson III

Sounds

2. Note that Cooper *s* is written under *m*: . Keep it the same size as *a* or *chay*; a large one means something else.

In *lowest,* the superlative *est* is added to the already complete word, and therefore the *o* must be written.

Theory

1. Long vowels sound just the way you say them:

a	bait	mate
e	beat	meet
i	bite	might
o	boat	moat
u	butte	mute

Exceptions to this theory are: ate at, eat et, oat ot.

2. Words are composed of one or more syllables. In words of two or more syllables, more emphasis is given to one syllable than to another. This emphasis, usually expressed vocally in a higher tone, is known as the accent. Test your knowledge of accent: apple—APPle; appraise—aPPRAISE; denial—deNIal; calendar—CALendar; career—caREER; affidavit—AffiDAvit. The last word has two accents—the first syllable has a secondary accent.
2. Note: Short vowel sounds are illustrated in the following words: bat, met, fit, lot, and hut. Short vowels with *l, m, n,* or *x* sound very like the letter you'll be writing, especially with *e*: elevate, exit, emanate, enamel. Tip: Write *x* without a pen-lift: write the first loop of an *n* n, then write a *c* c : x.
3. Some words with unaccented initial vowels may be written with the initial vowels in order to avoid confusion with similarly written words: attach atc, touch tc; attack atc, take tc. Write the initial vowel when there is a secondary accent on the first syllable: afdvt.

True Suffixes

1. This past tense symbol is called *suffix*. It is placed close to the end of the last letter or symbol of a word.
2. Could you use this suffix with the word *family*? No!
3. Call this symbol *ing*. It is a short upward stroke from left to right which starts letter high.

Memory Words

11. *Note* would be confused with *know* if it were written according to theory.

LESSON IV

Sounds

1. The longhand spelling determines the use of *s* and *z* except for the sounds of *ize* and *poze* which come in a later lesson.

gaze rose doze tease

2. = sounds of *ld* and *lt*; it is called *elt*. The stroke goes up more than out, and the tail of the symbol is parallel to the writing line.

sold
melt
*golden
resulted
quilt
*mildew
fold
weld
belt
child
*seldom
guilt

*Note that it is necessary to have a pen-lift in the middle of these words.

3. = sound of *ow*; it is called *ow*. The stroke through the *o* is downward from left to right.

south
now
mouth
allow
douse
chow
bow
mouse
foul

Theory

1. *r* following a vowel is indicated by underscoring either the vowel or the preceding consonant. The underscore stroke goes from left to right. It is written close under its letter or symbol.
   (a) If a word begins with a vowel plus *r* sound *in the same syllable,* or if a word ends in a long vowel plus *r* sound, write the vowel and underscore it.

iron	in	door	do	urban	ubn
earn	en	area	aa	ordain	odn
fire	fi	rare	ra	pair	pa
cheer	Ce	pure	pu	fear	fe
But: iris	irs.	erase	rs	arrive	riv

   (b) In every other case, omit the vowel and underscore the preceding consonant.

sever	sv	jobber	jb	manner	mn
mortal	mtl	expert	xpt	solder	sd
summer	sm	labor	lb	worth	wf
former	fm	firm	fm	folder	fd

Suffix

i = *-ire* in words of two or more syllables.

require	rqi	entire	nti	desire	dsi
attire	ati	acquire	aqi	expire	xpi
retire	rti	empire	mpi	satire	sti

Memory Words

1. *—o* more
2. *y* year, yearly
3. *ll* little
4. *cz* cause, because
5. *og* old
6. *rp* report
7. *bf* before
8. *vs* advice, advise, advisable, advisory
9. *o* circular
10. *l* letter
11. *bs* business
12. *o* over
13. *C* customer
14. *n* nor, near, nearly
15. *od* order, orderly
16. *nv* never

Plurals, Possessives, and Third Person Singular

Add *s* to a word that ends in a letter.

laughs *lfs* riches *res* man's *—ns* pillows *plos*

Add a tick to a word that ends in a symbol. A tick is a short downward stroke that crosses the end of the symbol.

pours *po* insults *nst* cows *co* meetings *—t*

A few symbols are doubled: examples will be given when the symbols are introduced.

See Practice Guidelines for an alternate way of dealing with some Memory Words.

Vocabulary

1. course
2. desire
3. sour
4. finest
5. folded
6. diameter
7. material
8. pattern
9. record
10. empire
11. listened
12. nearly
13. orlon
14. wrappers
15. resign
16. their
17. north
18. worked
19. error
20. year
21. results
22. severe
23. letters
24. keeping
25. churches
26. essay
27. cease
28. iris
29. court
30. orbit
31. leather
32. order
33. elevator
34. bolts
35. sold
36. because
37. urchin
38. towels
39. per
40. child
41. effort
42. neatly
43. latest
44. radiator

45. choir
46. cold
47. allows
48. fairer

Phrase Drill

1. at first sight
2. before you are
3. day or so
4. this model
5. in order
6. we have never
7. each of these
8. little or no
9. mail order
10. he is now
11. with this firm
12. to which I am
13. in due course
14. some of these

Lesson Review

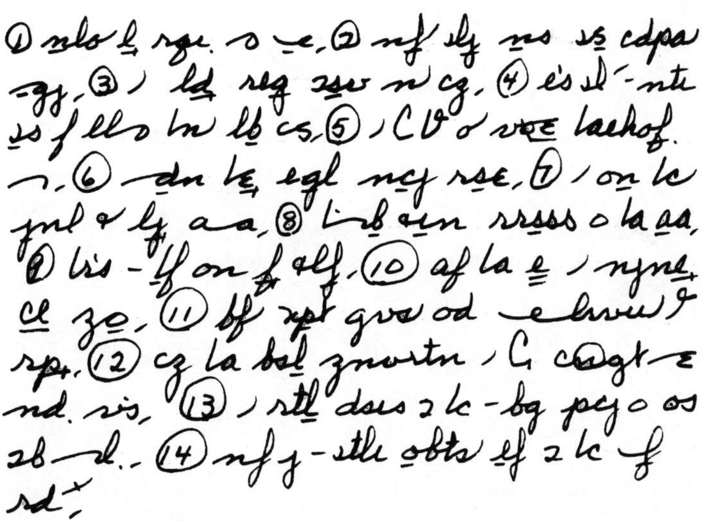

1. Nearly all of the letters required more work. 2. Neither the soldier nor his sister could pay the mortgage. 3. The leaders are eager to serve in the cause. 4. He's selling an entire series for little more than the labor cost. 5. The customer told of the voucher that he had offered him. 6. Modern teachers eagerly encourage research. 7. The owner took the journal and the ledgers away. 8. Timber and iron are resources of that area. 9. There's a tariff on furs and leather. 10. After that error the engineer's career was over. 11. Before the expert gives the order, he will review the old reports. 12. Because that business letter was never written, the customers cannot get much needed advice. 13. The retailer desires to take a big package of circulars to be mailed. 14. In this age a satellite orbits the earth to take weather readings.

Practice Guidelines for Lesson IV

Sounds

1. We have already used this rule with the words *as, has,* and *does.*
2. Check your practice of *elt*: avoid an initial stroke that stretches out to the right () or a final stroke that tends to the vertical ().  is correct. Note where the underscore is put in relation to *elt*: elder . The pen-lift in the middle of a word will also be needed with other symbols that end above the writing line.

Theory

1. **(a)** Note the phrase "in the same syllable." In the fifth line of examples, the initial vowels are not in the same syllables as the *r* sounds.

Plurals, Possessives, and Third Person Singular

A Memory Word that ends in a letter may add a joined tick instead of adding *s*. Keep the tick *short*. In transcribing, the tick signals a Memory Word: notes  notice  ; businesses  basis;  assistants  assistance  .

Vocabulary

3. Note the joined stroke in which the underscore goes from right to left without a pen-lift after writing *ow*.
5. Note the position of the suffix. 12, 33, 42, 43, 44: Here suffix endings are added to the basic words in which *t* is omitted after a long vowel. 19 and 48: note the double underscores. To make the plural of 19, use the tick:  .

Phrase Drill

No word can be joined to a symbol that ends above the line: Weld the metal.  When phrasing words ending with *m*, do not put the first letter of the next word under the *m*. See 14. Remember that phrasing is individual; some phrases will be more natural to you than others. Can you read your phrases readily?

Lesson Review

5. Note the joined strokes in *voucher*.

Speed Building: Lessons I–IV

Most people write longhand at about the same speed—from 30 to 35 words a minute. The secret of taking shorthand quickly, then, is to write continuously without pauses and hesitations and to write compactly.

The Speed Building sections can be most effective if you have the help of a friend or of a tape recorder. To build speed, you must take dictation, and that implies someone or something that dictates.

The words in the following drills are counted in groups of 20 standard words (28 syllables). These groupings are indicated by slashes. Use the table given below to determine dictation speed:

Words per minute (wpm)	Dictation time for every 20 words
40	30 seconds
50	24 seconds
60	20 seconds

To make your own tapes, first practice reading aloud the drill material until you are speaking at the speed you want. Start at the lowest speed and take 30 seconds to read to each slash. When you have established the pace to speak at 40 wpm, dictate to the tape recorder, checking the time carefully so that the tape produces the dictation speed you wish to practice.

The knack of coordinating your hearing with your writing develops with practice. When you first start to concentrate on speed, you are apt to feel a sense of pressure that is reflected in scrawly penmanship. Make yourself relax! The larger you write, the longer it takes. *Practice each sentence separately* before timing yourself. If you hesitated in writing any word, work on it until it is second nature to write it correctly. Push yourself to go faster while keeping your penmanship small and controlled.

The starting drill at 40 wpm is not concerned so much with speed as it is with good, compact penmanship. Read what you have written to be sure you are accurate.

Don't expect to make a dramatic jump in speed overnight. Your progress will depend on the amount of time you devote to practice.

Drill 1

Your name was put on our list of customers last year. We are eager to serve you. We have a new line of model/ kits designed to delight all from child to adult. The little metal tools you will need for each kit are in the box/ with the model. It is lots of fun to match up the model pieces. It will make you feel like a mechanic. Just/ follow the patterns step by step. If you get stuck, we have an expert to advise you. Let him give you aid. Do come to see us./

Drill 2

I have learned that a senate filibuster may kill the bill which is to reform the legal system and the courts./ I do not know what your expert will say on the merits of this bill, but such an effort would cheat citizens of/ their rights. I urge you to do what you can to see that all may have their say so that the bill can be fairly decided./

Drill 1

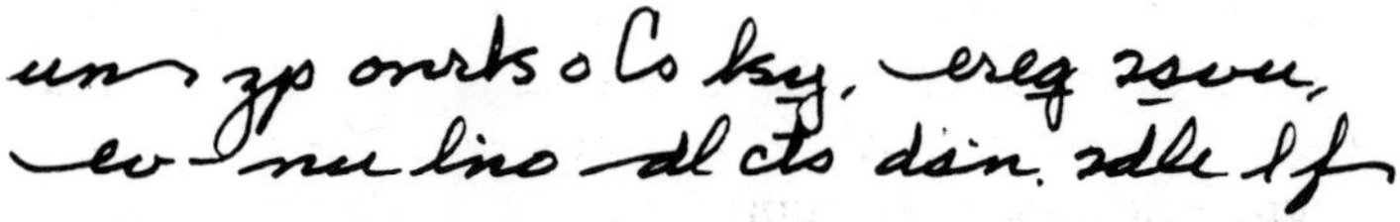

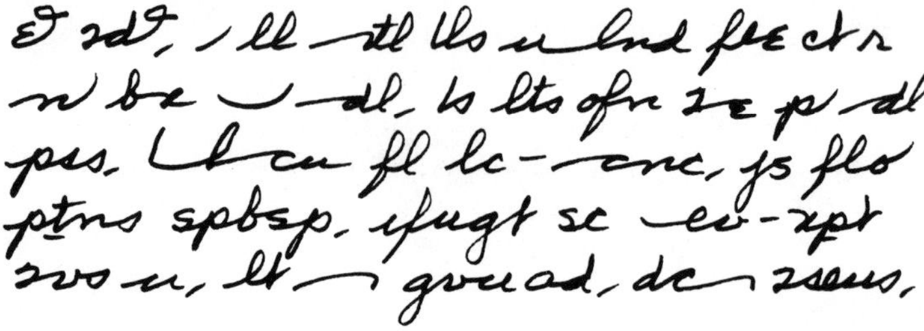

Drill 2

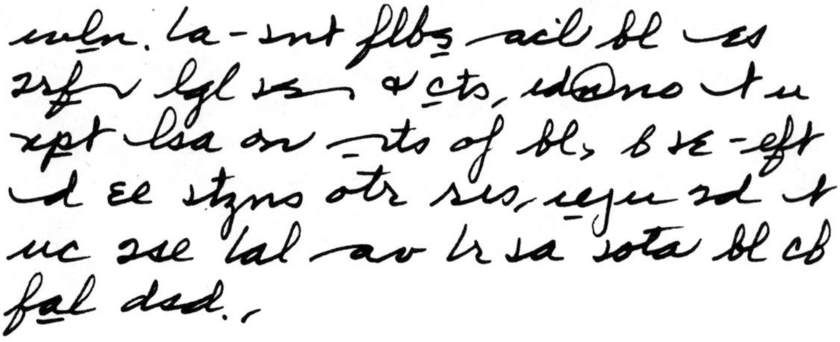

LESSON V

Sounds

1. = sounds of *sh* and *zh*; it is called *ish.* At the end of a word, the stroke ends to the left; otherwise, the stroke joining it to the next letter should trace the bottom of the symbol.

shut	leisure	cash
seizure	measure	ratio
she	machine	shelter

2. = sounds of *sk* and *skw* at the beginning of a word; in the middle or end of word, write

skip	basket	square
masquerade	scold	task

Theory

1. A consonant is overscored to indicate that the letter *r* immediately follows it. The overscore stroke goes from left to right; tall letters are cut by it and short letters are almost touched.

refrain	provide	treasure
program	proper	trial

When an *r* immediately follows a medial *t*, the *t* is crossed twice: once to cross the *t* and once as an overscore.

patron ptn metric stc citrus sts

Memory Words

1. ul until
2. d during
3. td today
4. to tomorrow
5. r where
6. tfn telephone
7. be believe, belief
8. ap appear, appearance, apparent, apparently
9. f from
10. L them
11. y why
12. S shall, ship
13. e here, hear
14. e. heard
15. nl only
16. ⓤ ask

Vocabulary

1. So shore
2. ps price
3. ts treasurer
4. ncs increased
5. rs. resulted
6. fa freight
7. pa prayer
8. rse receipt
9. So shower
10. sa straight
11. Ql skill
12. Sp shopper
13. snSn sunshine
14. Qo score
15. fnS finish
16. fSm freshman
17. c colder
18. slba celebrate

19. desk
20. opera
21. days
22. believes
23. drew
24. note
25. rescue
26. eager
27. fry
28. businesses
29. earnest
30. scarce
31. program
32. method
33. broken
34. treated
35. square
36. appear
37. solemn
38. over

Phrase Drill

1. above named
2. can become
3. should not say
4. if you wish
5. may be finished
6. I should have
7. do you wish
8. on schedule
9. do you believe
10. it shall be
11. can you appear
12. it was proved
13. he was afraid
14. you are hereby

Lesson Review

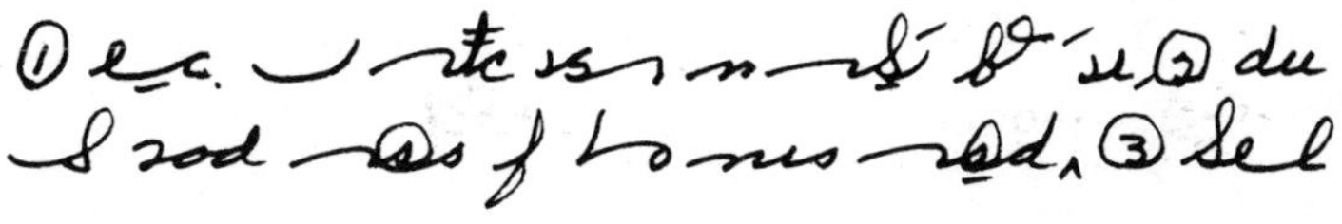

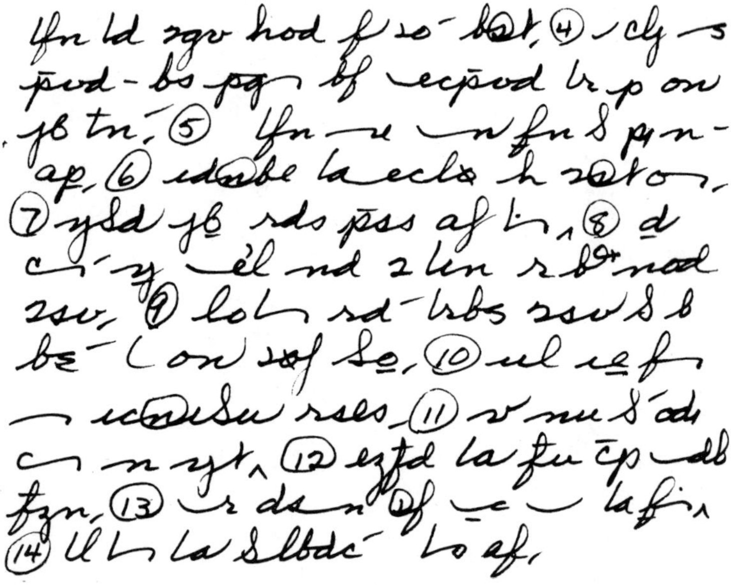

1. He worked with the metric system in measuring the building site. 2. Do you wish to order masks for tomorrow night's masquerade? 3. She will telephone today to give her order for the sewing basket. 4. The college must provide a business program before we can provide their people on-the-job training. 5. Telephone me when the foreign ship puts in an appearance. 6. I do not believe that we can allow her to ask it of him. 7. Why should the jobber reduce prices at this time? 8. During the coming year we'll need to tighten our belts in order to save. 9. All of them are doing their best to save the ship by beaching it on the south shore. 10. Until I hear from him, I cannot issue the receipts. 11. Have the new shipping orders come in yet? 12. He was afraid that the fruit crop would be frozen. 13. Where does one ask for work with that firm? 14. Tell them that the ship will be docking tomorrow afternoon.

Practice Guidelines for Lesson V

Sounds

1. If the joining stroke does not retrace the bottom of the symbol *ish,* you are writing a symbol that means something else: therefore  , not  or .
2. Note that  is not put under the  as in *masquerade.*

Theory

1. Note joined overscores in *program.*

Vocabulary

9. Another example of joined strokes without a pen-lift.

Lesson Review

8. The basic word is *tight* to which a suffix is added.

LESSON VI

Sounds

1. ` = final *y* with the sound of *e* when not in the sounds of *zy, ry, ety,* and *ity* and the true suffix *ly*. It is called final *y*. The stroke must be short, close to the top of the letter it follows, and go in a downward left-to-right direction. Double it for the plural.

remedy  silly  journeys 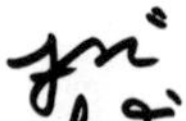
family  happy  faculty 

Theory

1. At the beginning of a word, *h* is omitted before long vowels and before *ow*.

hotel  howl  humor 
house  haven  how 

Exceptions: hay, hate  ; heat  ; high, height  ; hoe  ; hoot  ; hire  ; hair  .

2. *nd, nt, n, d,* and *t* are omitted after *ow*.

pound  county  gown 
crowd  out  fountain 

Memory Words

1. go, good, goods
2. taken
3. given
4. answer
5. those
6. bring
7. credit
8. dozen
9. receive, reception
10. into
11. office
12. realize, really
13. etc.
14. change
15. great, greatly
16. many, money
17. policy
18. care, careful, carefully

Capitalization

= capital letter: Tom , Alice , Susan

= all capitals: RESOLVED .

= capitalized initials: R. A. Mitchell

Ray Mitchell

Write the longhand *k* when it is an initial.

K. A. Smith , Kelley Ann Smith

Vocabulary

1. council
2. home
3. out
4. Betty

5. haven
6. trout
7. heat
8. warehouse
9. faculty
10. drought
11. risky
12. scowl
13. bountiful
14. sympathy
15. power
16. ground
17. about
18. sour
19. receives
20. around
21. brown
22. families
23. shout
24. down
25. loud
26. howl
27. count
28. courtesy
29. hope
30. early
31. town
32. silly
33. honey
34. hate
35. proud
36. how

Phrase Drill

1. about the
2. any more
3. I have received
4. out of order
5. to his credit
6. if you go
7. no doubt
8. from you
9. to my account
10. may we hope
11. account book

12. nnics in any case
13. onobx on or about
14. so-' so many
15. dube do you believe
16. nul in your letter

Lesson Review

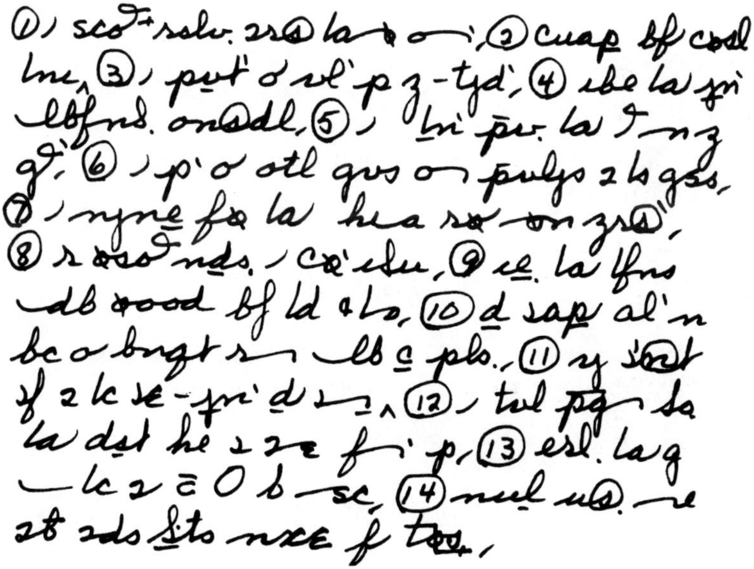

1. The stockholders resolved to risk that amount of money. 2. Can you appear before the council tonight? 3. The poverty of the valley people was a tragedy. 4. I believe that the journey will be finished on schedule. 5. The attorney proved that the old man was guilty. 6. The policy of the hotel gives home privileges to its guests. 7. The engineer found that the highway around the mountain was risky. 8. Our household endorsed the county issue. 9. I heard that the telephones would be out of order both today and tomorrow. 10. During his appearance the alley in back of the banquet room will be carefully policed. 11. Why isn't it

safe to take such a journey during the summer? 12. The travel program showed that the desert heat is too much for many people. 13. He realized that the goods were taken to the credit office by mistake. 14. In your letter you asked me to bring two dozen shirts in exchange for the trousers.

Practice Guidelines for Lesson VI

Sounds

1. The exceptions *zy, ry, ety,* and *ity* are suffixes you will learn later.

Theory

1. *Who* is not included in the list of exceptions because it is a Memory Word to be given in a later lesson.
2. Note the joined strokes in *crowd.*

Memory Words

5. If *those* were not a Memory Word, it could be confused with *these.*
9. Most Memory Words are among the 2000 most frequently used words; all are within the 5000 most frequently used. Therefore, many derivatives of Memory Words are not listed because they are used less often. (In this context a derivative is a word formed from the original by adding a suffix.) In this example, the derivative *receivable* is not included. However, in most instances, you can let the Memory Words represent their derivatives too.

10. The second loop of *n* becomes the top curve of *2* which finishes below the writing line.

Vocabulary

3 and 36. Both are written the same way.

8. Whenever you have two words joined to make one word, treat each part of the combination as a separate word: in this case the *h* of "hold" is therefore omitted.

Lesson Review

14. The prefix *ex* is added to the Memory Word *change*. Note how important that dot is in *shirts;* otherwise it could be transcribed *shorts*.

LESSON VII

Sounds

 = *nd* and *nt* sounds; it is called *ent.*

island		ancient		extended	
kinds		cylinder		rental	

Theory

1. A consonant is slashed to indicate that *l* immediately follows it; the slash slants downward from left to right. *Ent* cannot be slashed.

sleepy		samples		chronicle	
thistle		plant		muscle	
trouble		handle		cloud	

2. *t* is omitted when it immediately follows *c, p, x,* and *f,* except after the prefix *ex.*

kept	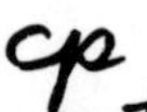	factor		text	
extend	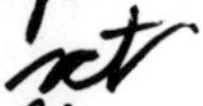	direct		rectify	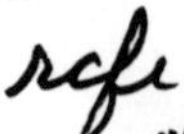
lift		extol	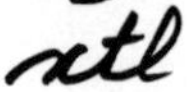	deflect	

Suffix

¢ = *-ical.*

technical lcn¢ musical -s¢ physical fs¢
medical -d¢ rhetorical rt¢ historical hs¢

Memory Words

Many Memory Words are formed by writing in shorthand the abbreviations of the longhand.

ap = appl. = apply, application, applicable
df = def. = definite, definitely, definition
dv = dev. = develop, development
n¢ = encl. = enclose, enclosure
ex = ex. = except, exception, exceptional, exceptionally
xp = exper. = experience
jn = gen. = general, generally
-p = imp. = import, important, importance
nq = inq. = inquire, inquiry
-t = mat. = matter
-x = max. = maximum
-n = min. = minimum
ps = pers. = person, personal, personally
ps = pos. = possible, possibly, possibility
p̄n = prin. = principle, principal

p̄b = prob. = probable, probably, probability
p̄p = prop. = proper, properly, property
pb = pub. = public, publicity
rf = ref. = refer, reference
rg = reg. = regular, regularly, regulation
s̲v = serv. = service, servicing
sv = sev. = several
sc = suc. = succeed, success, successful, successfully
sg = sug. = suggest, suggestion

Numbers

1. Write numbers in digits, except *one.*

   Buy two ties, four shirts, and one suit.

   b 2 tis, 4 S̲ts & n su.

2. Dollars are written on the writing line, and cents above the line.

$1.69 1^{69} $203.60 203^{60} 45¢ ^{45} $1,348.21 1348^{21}

3. dollar D hundred H thousand T million ⌒

   He owes hundreds of dollars. eos HoD.

   It cost ten million dollars. cs 10⌒D.

Vocabulary

1. acs acts
2. rsd resident
3. ml mailing
4. pb public

5. physical
6. northern
7. draft
8. human
9. writing
10. envy
11. handle
12. black
13. slight
14. client
15. elect
16. worse
17. floor
18. effect
19. solemn
20. deduct
21. gifts
22. slide
23. semester
24. favorite
25. remainder
26. sufficient
27. clipping
28. dividend
29. desirable
30. parents
31. battles
32. protest
33. payable
34. whistle
35. tentacle
36. grown
37. medical
38. repair
39. textile
40. plenty
41. orange
42. happy
43. close
44. soft
45. honesty
46. chapter

Phrase Drill

1. as you will
2. at all events
3. I am directed
4. he could find

5.  she cannot
6. 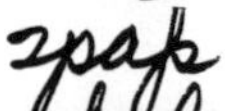 to pay these
7. 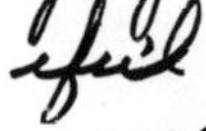 if you'll
8.  of any kind
9. 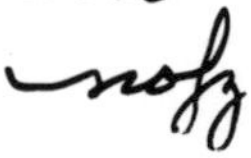 one of those
10.  in reference
11.  good for you
12. 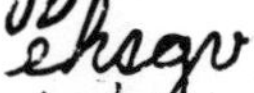 he has given
13. 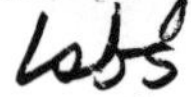 it is best
14.  you don't

Lesson Review

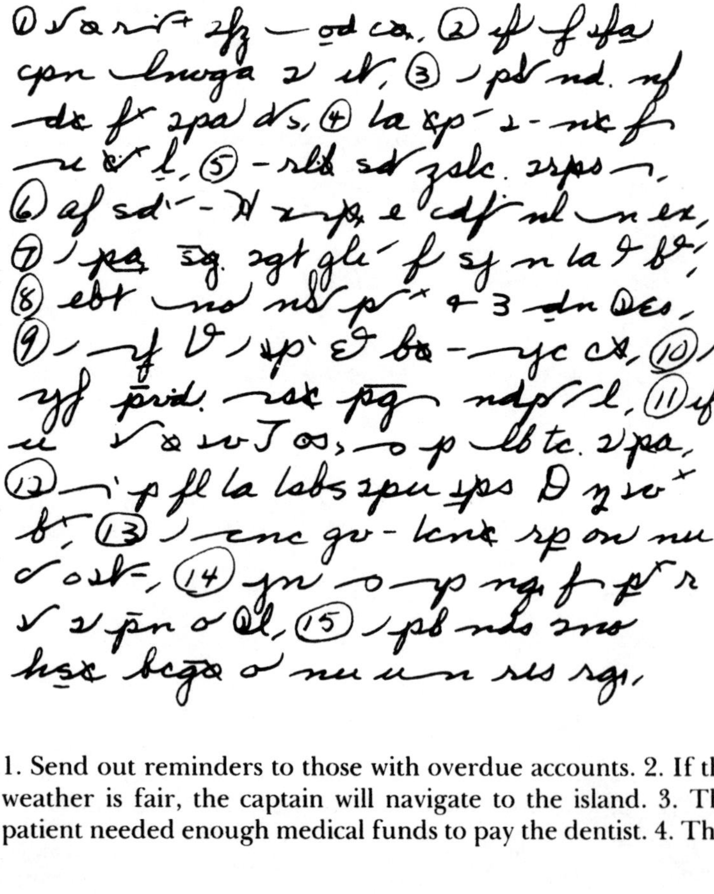

1. Send out reminders to those with overdue accounts. 2. If the weather is fair, the captain will navigate to the island. 3. The patient needed enough medical funds to pay the dentist. 4. That

clipping is an enclosure from my client's letter. 5. A reliable student was selected to replace him. 6. After studying a hundred examples, he could find only one exception. 7. The players struggled to get good lighting for the stage in that old building. 8. He bought one of the ancient paintings and three modern sketches. 9. The mother told the sleepy child about a magic castle. 10. The youth provided the musical program independently. 11. If you send out several thousand circulars, more people will be attracted to the play. 12. Many people feel that it is best to put your surplus funds into savings bonds. 13. The mechanic gave a technical report on the new kind of cylinder. 14. Generally the more important inquiries from parents are sent to the principal of the school. 15. The public needs to know the historical background of the new human rights regulations.

Practice Guidelines for Lesson VII

Sounds

Ent always starts from the writing line. Plural: use the tick. Note the placement of the underscore and *suffix. It* cannot be overscored: tendril  *Ent* rarely begins a word: intent , indolent 

Theory

1. When a slash comes at the beginning or middle of a word, finish the word without a pen-lift and then return to make the slash: plant 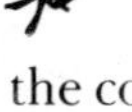, deflate 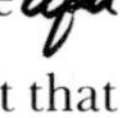. In *thistle, muscle,* and similar words, the consonant that is sounded is slashed if there is no vowel between the consonant and *l.* Tick this symbol to make the plural.

Memory Words

Additional Memory Words based on abbreviations will be given in a later lesson.

Numbers

3. Rarely will you need to indicate the plural of these Memory Words: the sentence structure informs you.

Vocabulary

Compare 15 with 18: without the initial *e, effect* might be confused with *fact* in some contexts. In context, *elect* is unlikely to be confused with other readings.

Phrase Drill

14. You have your choice of writing *don't* either  or  . The same will be true of *can't, won't, isn't,* etc.

LESSON VIII

Sounds

1. = sound of *sp*.

space — whisper — split

clasp — specimen — inspire

spread — despair — spend

2. = sound of *ah*.

father — balmy — wasp

calm — wad — salami

= sound of *aw*.

saw — audit — laws

talk — caught — daughter

= sound of *ah* + *r*.

car — partner — army

Mars — sharp — sergeant

The check is not used when there is an *o* in the longhand spelling.

Prefixes and Suffixes

1. = true prefix *fore*.

forenoon — forecast — foresight

Some Memory Words can be used as prefixes and suffixes:

2. S = *ship.*

starship sˆs   shipmate Sa   scholarship Qls

3. o̲ = *over.*

overdue o̲d   stopover spo̲   overcome o̲c

Memory Words

1. ⁄ end
2. np envelope
3. f friend, friendly
4. b able, ability
5. pˊ part, party
6. sf self
7. c collect, collection
8. ax accept, acceptable, acceptance
9. -y manage, manager
10. cˇ charge
11. xp expect
12. ev ever, every
13. x̄v however
14. f other
15. -f month, monthly
16. bh behind
17. -p please, pleasure, pleasant
18. f through

Vocabluary

1. ˇts artist
2. hdlˊ handling
3. Qf scarf
4. fhd forehead
5. dls wholesome
6. -sbˊ assembly
7. fls false
8. nˊ any

9. target
10. car
11. sending
12. shipyard
13. whisper
14. window
15. forgive
16. senator
17. capable
18. forego
19. typical
20. similar
21. private
22. accurate
23. foreman
24. terribly
25. friendly
26. cynical
27. popovers
28. foretell
29. testimony
30. overcome
31. frequent
32. anyone
33. hire
34. call
35. wasp
36. awful
37. caught
38. auditor
39. season
40. father
41. icicle
42. talk
43. laws
44. thrown

Phrase Drill

1. to eliminate
2. civil laws
3. this clause
4. of importance
5. call upon you
6. will be able
7. you must bring
8. I will collect
9. he will hire
10. to accept the

11.		to bring in	17.		to develop
12.		for collection	18.		I expect you
13.		he will ask	19.		each other
14.		that is the	20.		it was sent
15.		please advise	21.		of value
16.		can change the	22.		this month

Lesson Review

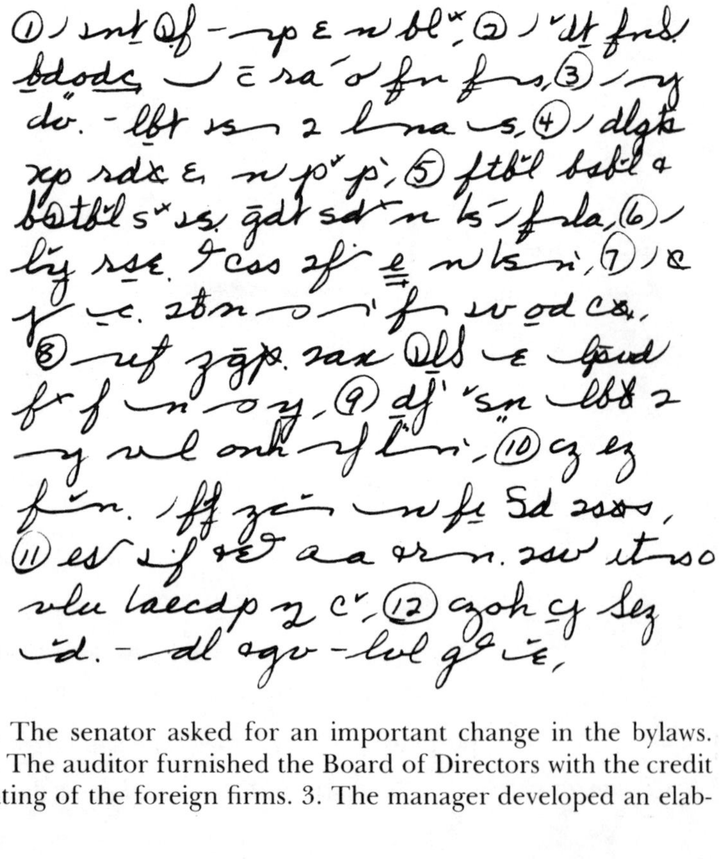

1. The senator asked for an important change in the bylaws. 2. The auditor furnished the Board of Directors with the credit rating of the foreign firms. 3. The manager developed an elab-

orate system to eliminate waste. 4. The delegates expect radical changes in the party's policy. 5. Football, baseball, and basketball stars assisted the graduate students in testing the formula. 6. The lawyer researched old cases to find errors in the testimony. 7. The collection agent worked to bring in more money from several overdue accounts. 8. My friend was greatly pleased to accept the scholarship which will provide the funds for one more year. 9. Dorothy Austin will be able to manage very well on her monthly alimony. 10. Because he was forewarned, the father was calm when the fire spread to his house. 11. He sent his wife and child away and remained to save the items of value that he could put into the car. 12. Because of her courage, she was awarded a medal and given a lovely gold watch.

Practice Guidelines for Lesson VIII

Sounds

1. Note how the large Cooper *s* is overscored and slashed.
2. The *l* is silent in words like *calm, psalm, walk,* and *talk.*

Unless a word starts with a check (art: ), write the word or phrase without a pen-lift and then check it. Tick the check to make the plural. This is one of the few rules where you have to be aware of spelling as well as sound. Although many words with *o* in the spelling sound the same, the check is not used: sought  , caught  .

Prefixes and Suffixes

Just as the suffix is a word ending, a prefix is a word beginning.

Lesson Review

2. A single capitalization sign under the *phrase* "Board of Directors" is sufficient.

Speed Building: Lessons I–VIII

Remember: to write 40 wpm, dictation time to each slash is 30 seconds; 50 wpm = 24 seconds; 60 wpm = 20 seconds.

Before timing yourself, write each sentence repeatedly until you do it smoothly and without hesitation. Concentrate on relaxing so that your penmanship is controlled and compact.

Speed Drill

In reference to your letter of three days ago, please allow me to suggest a different plan. I/ realize that there have been too many inaccurate news accounts about the space shuttle. I believe that these are due/ to our efforts to delay the publicity release. Why don't we develop a series of relevant news/ events over the next six weeks which will build to the same sort of climax that we had intended in the original plan?/ Your staff would be feeding right answers to the public rather than having to deny the mistaken imaginings/ that have been made about the project. Let's end all the speculating and see that only facts are in the news/.

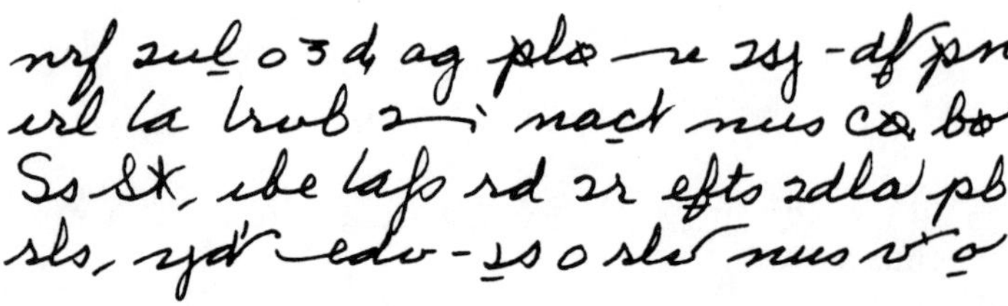

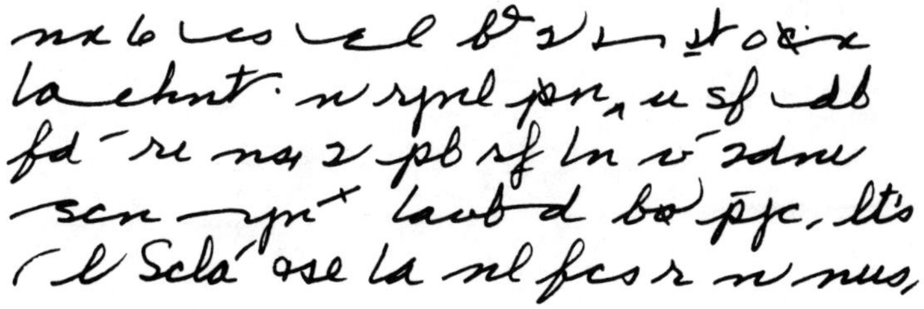

LESSON IX

Sounds

1. = sounds of *shun, ch'n,* and *zhun*: it is called *shun*.

ocean	Christian	version
coercion	patrician	promotion
fashions	bastion	decision

2. = *nk* sound; it is called *ank*. It cannot be slashed.

tank	drink	uncle
trinket	bank	skunk

Prefixes and Suffixes

1. = *self* as prefix and suffix.

selfish	myself	selfsame

2. = *-ment*. This symbol is not joined to the letter or symbol that precedes it.

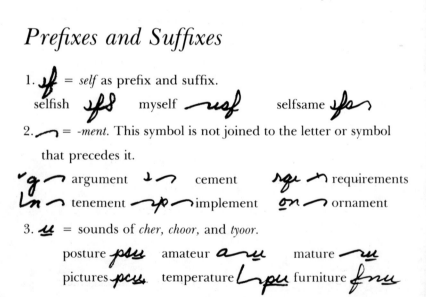

argument	cement	requirements
tenement	implement	ornament

3. = sounds of *cher, choor,* and *tyoor*.

posture	amateur	mature
pictures	temperature	furniture

Memory Words

1. state, statement
2. sure, surely, assure, assurance
3. prepare, preparation
4. difficult, difficulty
5. inform, information
6. secretary, secretarial
7. departure, department
8. secure, security
9. under, understand
10. understood
11. consider, considerable, consideration
12. help, helpful
13. individual, individually
14. thing
15. anything
16. nothing
17. something
18. everything
19. thank, thanks
20. number
21. position
22. purchase
23. sale

Vocabulary

1. capture
2. without
3. dutiful
4. culture
5. smaller
6. mature
7. away
8. states
9. why
10. uncle
11. signature
12. vacation
13. physician
14. management

15. thanking
16. lecture
17. action
18. station
19. leisure
20. mission
21. himself
22. posture
23. slowly
24. venture
25. failure
26. section
27. feature
28. version
29. simply
30. reason
31. cure
32. think
33. figure
34. trunk
35. bank
36. trust
37. rank
38. mother
39. smoke
40. future
41. drink
42. fixtures
43. fundamental
44. changeable
45. affection
46. detection
47. difficult
48. wonderful
49. temptation
50. endorsement
51. departure
52. population
53. foundation
54. relations

Phrase Drill

1. in this action
2. it was written
3. he will surely
4. those you seek

5. it would help
6. in preparation
7. will you note
8. please inform
9. was readily
10. to evaluate
11. can you think
12. he is sure
13. your judgment
14. you can help
15. in addition
16. is not right
17. large number
18. no charge
19. after seeing
20. too much

Lesson Review

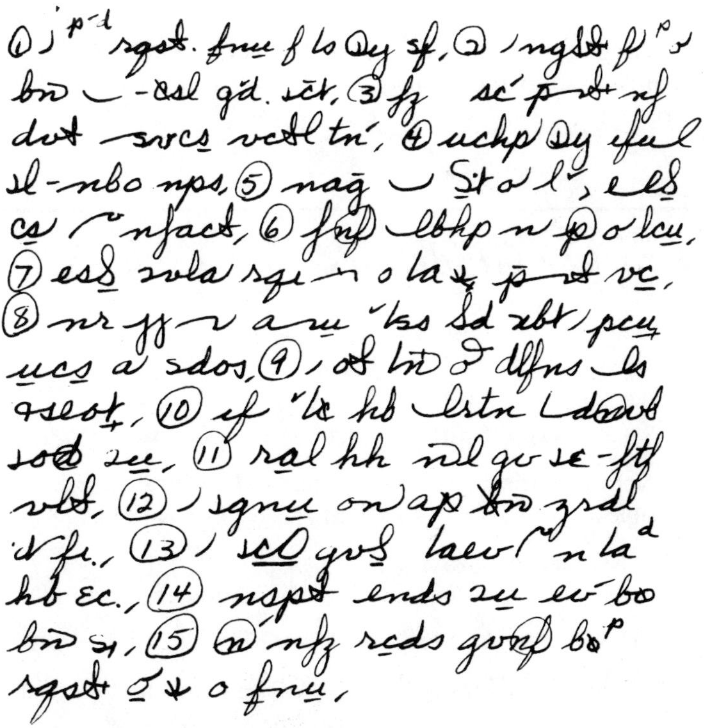

1. The purchasing department requisitioned furniture for its secretarial staff. 2. The negotiations for the purchase of the bank were a closely guarded secret. 3. Those seeking promotions in this division must have considerable vocational training. 4. You can help the secretary if you will seal a number of envelopes. 5. In agreement with the spirit of the law, he will surely consider the individual in this action. 6. This information will be helpful in the preparation of the lecture. 7. He is sure to evaluate the requirements of that sales promotion very carefully. 8. In our judgment the amateur artists should exhibit the pictures under consideration at the studios. 9. The ocean tanks hold dolphins, whales, and sea otters. 10. If the article had been well written it would not have been so difficult to understand. 11. Rarely had her uncle given such a thoughtful evaluation. 12. The signature on the application blank was readily identified. 13. The security officer gave assurance that every individual in that department had been checked. 14. In his position he needs to understand everything about bank statements. 15. Nothing in those records gave information about purchase requisitions or the sale of furniture.

Practice Guidelines for Lesson IX

Sounds

1. *Shun* is written with an angle, not a loop: not .

   Note that the tick is used to make the plural. It is possible—and quick—to extend the backstroke of *shun* to cross the *t* in *patrician.*
2. Note how *uncle* is written. Another example: wrinkle 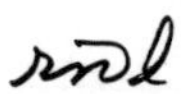. Plural: use the tick: sinks . *Ank* is extended to overscore the preceding letters in *drink* and

trinket. The rule to omit *t* after *c* holds for *ank*: sanctify  .

Prefixes and Suffixes

2.  *must* be disjoined from that which precedes it; however, you may add to *ment* a sound that follows: supplemental  .
3. Notice that *t* is always in the longhand spelling of these three sounds.

Vocabulary

27. *Feature* includes the *e* to avoid confusion with *future*.

LESSON X

Sounds

1. ´ = sound of *ing* at the end of nouns of two or more syllables. It is identical in name and formation to the true suffix *ing*.

   ceiling sl´ stocking sc´ pudding pd´

2. [illegible] = *ng* when it is not in the suffix *ing*. It is not used when the *g* has a *j* sound, as in *fringe:* frj. Do not slash.

   hung [illegible] ring [illegible] single [illegible]
   belongs [illegible] finger [illegible] tangle [illegible]

   When a *w* sound follows [illegible], omit it.

   lingual [illegible] language [illegible] sanguine [illegible]

3. , = *ss* at the *end* of a word. Double it to make the plural.

   mass [illegible] possess ps, stressed [illegible]
   brass [illegible] class [illegible] glasses [illegible]

   When a suffix that requires a pen-lift is added to a word which ends in *ss,* use the comma before the suffix: embarrassment [illegible], dressing [illegible]; but: classify [illegible].

Theory

In words of three or more syllables, *n* is omitted when preceded by short *e*. This cannot occur in the first or last syllable.

messenger passenger extension
davenport penitent nitrogen

Memory Words

1. separate, separately
2. thorough, thoroughly
3. yesterday
4. regret
5. who
6. satisfy
7. satisfaction
8. approve, approval
9. paper
10. newspaper
11. store
12. favor, favorable, favorably
13. attention
14. Mr.
15. Mrs.
16. together
17. request
18. themselves
19. ourselves
20. women
21. men
22. use, useful
23. appreciate, appreciative, appreciation

Vocabulary

1. danger
2. long
3. class
4. nature

5. harass
6. across
7. among
8. sing
9. abrupt
10. banjo
11. along
12. hanger
13. kings
14. tongue
15. arm
16. bungalow
17. selfless
18. kingdom
19. guessed
20. message
21. pudding
22. fortress
23. bearing
24. hopeless
25. inspire
26. strange
27. mingle
28. progress
29. ceiling
30. cringe
31. different
32. intention
33. youngster
34. retention
35. strength
36. processes
37. intensify
38. invention
39. stockings
40. impresses
41. harmony
42. extension
43. mission
44. wing

Phrase Drill

1. for so long
2. among the
3. of his work
4. next thing
5. long ago
6. my pleasure

7. will favor
8. that we refer
9. if you approve
10. it is possible
11. I appreciate
12. who is it
13. thorough study
14. your request

Lesson Review

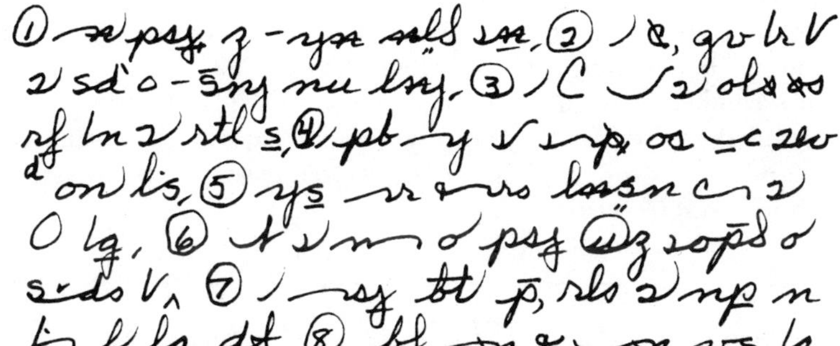

1. Among the passengers was a young English singer. 2. The class gave their attention to the study of a strange new language. 3. The customer went to the wholesale house rather than to the retail store. 4. The publicity manager sent samples of his work

to every department on the list. 5. Yesterday Mr. and Mrs. Langston came to the office together. 6. What is the name of the passenger who was so appreciative of her ward's attention? 7. The messenger brought the press release to the newspaper in time for the late edition. 8. Both men and women have stated that they are favorably impressed with the new service. 9. The decorator is satisfied with her selection of fabric for the old davenport. 10. Would you consider it wrong of me if I were to ask you to store newspapers for the school's paper drive? 11. He appreciated the good use that has been made of his text in the English classes. 12. She was embarrassed to find that she had brought the wrong glasses. 13. The architect noted that the upstairs ceiling would have to be replaced. 14. The secretary regretted that she had to refuse her boss's request. 15. Because the author was thorough in his research, the editor was not able to find a single error.

Practice Guidelines for Lesson X

Sounds

2. The bar through the *n* is parallel to the writing line. Plural: use the tick: songs  .

Theory

When a basic word ends in *ent* followed by a suffix that does not absorb the sound of *t*, or in *end*, it often seems more natural to use the *ent* symbol rather than the omission of *en* rule: *incidental*  or  , *expenditure*  or  ; however: inten*tion*  . This rule completes the Theory lessons.

Memory Words

22. Think of this as an open *u*.

Vocabulary

32, 34, and 42 all use the shortcut of crossing the *t* with the backstroke of *shun*.

Lesson Review

Remember that phrasing is individual. The test: Can you read your phrases easily?

7. Usually *edition* would require the initial *e* to prevent it from being confused with *addition*. However, in the context of this sentence, initial *e* doesn't seem necessary.

LESSON XI

Prefixes and Suffixes

1. u = the true prefix *un*

unfair ufa unhappy uhp unjust ujs
unlike ulc untried uti. undecided udsd

2. v = *-sive,* and *-tive*

negative ngv exclusive xclv relative rlv
extensive xtv executive xcv massive —v

3. u = *under* as prefix and suffix

undergo ug thereunder tru underneath unf
undertake utc undersized usz. hereunder eu

4. pd = *-position*

supposition spd proposition ppd deposition dpd

5. d = *dis-*

dispatch dpc disgrace dgs dismal dml
display dpa dislocate dlca discourage dcj

6. ʻo = *auto-*

autogyro ʻojo autocrat ʻocrt automate ʻo—a
autopsy ʻopsi autocracy ʻocsi autonomy ʻonmi

Memory Words

Days:

1. Sunday
2. Monday
3. Tuesday
4. Wednesday
5. Thursday
6. Friday
7. Saturday

Months:

1. January
2. February
3. March
4. April
5. May
6. June
7. July
8. August
9. September
10. October
11. November
12. December

Vocabulary

1. descriptive
2. uneven
3. automotive
4. discern
5. defensive
6. progressive
7. discuss
8. motive
9. supposition
10. unreal
11. dispatch
12. autocracy
13. dispute
14. proposition
15. unused
16. tentative
17. automation
18. dismal
19. unworthy
20. attractive
21. autonomy
22. discharge
23. understudy
24. offensive

25. unknown
26. undergo
27. disgusted
28. undergrowth
29. discretion
30. extensive
31. disable
32. underquote
33. spring
34. January

Phrase Drill

1. next Thursday
2. we are unable
3. were sent
4. are you sure
5. in reference
6. it was understood
7. was used
8. please ship the
9. to rescue the
10. on this copy
11. will disrupt
12. it is useful

Lesson Review

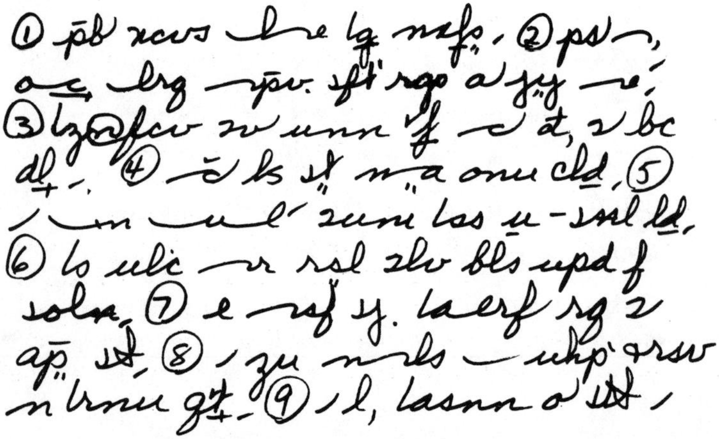

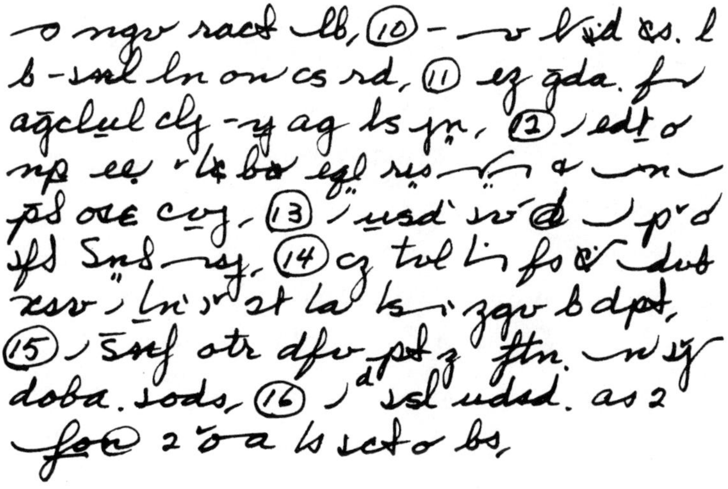

1. Probably the executives will meet together next Thursday. 2. Possibly the mass of workers will require improved safety regulations at the January meeting. 3. It was not effective to have the unknown author make the address to the book dealers. 4. Mark the last Saturday in May on your calendar. 5. The women were unwilling to unite themselves under a single leader. 6. It is unlike Mr. Russell to leave bills unpaid for so long. 7. He himself suggested that we refer the request to the April session. 8. The zoo animals were unhappy and restive in their new quarters. 9. The less that is known of the situation, the more negative the reaction will be. 10. A massive landslide closed all but a single lane on the coast road. 11. He was graduated from the agricultural college a year ago last June. 12. The editor of the newspaper used the article about the Equal Rights Amendment and the women were appreciative of such coverage. 13. The understudy is having difficulty with the part of the selfish Spanish messenger. 14. Because travel time for his client would have been excessive, the attorney saw to it that the testimony was given by deposition. 15. The strength of their defensive position was threatened when the sergeant disobeyed his orders. 16. The department is still undecided as to whether or not to automate its section of the business.

Practice Guidelines for Lesson XI

Prefixes

5. The addition of a prefix does not affect how the basic word is written; therefore a prefix is not slashed or scored: disrupt , dislodge 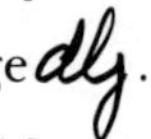.
6. *Auto* may be used alone as a Memory Word. Note that  is used even when the pronunciation of *o* is a short vowel, as in *autopsy* or *autonomy*.

Vocabulary

4. Since the prefix cannot be underscored, this word requires you to write out the second syllable: dis*cern* .

Lesson Review

2. Because the *t* in *safety* does not immediately follow the *f*, it must be written.

LESSON XII

Sounds

1. ⏐ = sound of *-ns*. Add a small *s* to make the plural. Call it *ens*.

cadence *cdˢ*	fences *fˢˢ*	offense *fˢ*
vacancy *vcˢ*	prince *pˢ*	valance *vlˢ*
leniency *lnˢ*	residence *rsdˢ*	resilience *rslˢ*

2. 𝓧 = sounds of *shul* and *zhul*.

partial *pˢ*	casual *cˢ*	officials *fˢ*
potential *ptˢ*	visual *vˢ*	social *sˢ*
artificial *lcfˢ*	initial *nˢ*	credentials *cdˢ*

3. *ₙ* = sound of *-ry*.

scenery *snₙ*	salary *slₙ*	worried *ₙ*
primary *prₙ*	temporary *Lₙ*	machinery *šnₙ*
factory *fcₙ*	stationery *stₙ*	theory *ₙ*

4. ō = *oy*. Call it *oy*. It is treated like 𝓧. See Practice Guidelines.

noise *nōs*	enjoys *njō*	royal *rōl*
spoiled *sōl*	loin *lō*	voyage *vōy*
poison *pōsn*	hoist *ōs*	embroidery *brōy*

Memory Words

1. publish, publication
2. company, accompany
3. include, inclusive, inclusion
4. copy
5. standard, standardization
6. glad, gladly
7. market, marketing
8. advance, advancement
9. recognize, recognition
10. special, specially, especially
11. satisfactory, satisfactorily
12. reply
13. automobile
14. acknowledge, acknowledgment
15. question
16. nature, natural, naturally
17. government, governmental
18. supply
19. appointment
20. disappointment
21. between
22. expense, expensive
23. register, registration

Vocabulary

1. unsavory
2. dense
3. story
4. romance
5. social
6. essence
7. initial
8. primary
9. despair
10. inspire
11. literary
12. sciences

13.	bō	boy	31.	ˇbty	arbitrary
14.	ōl'	oily	32.	dfˢ	difference
15.	clny	culinary	33.	nōˢ-	announcement
16.	—ˢ	immense	34.	nōˢ	annoyance
17.	Eōs	choice	35.	lˇy	laundry
18.	dcy	directory	36.	vcy	victory
19.	vōj	voyage	37.	jō	joint
20.	tō	toys	38.	dpsy	dispensary
21.	dˢ-	dancing	39.	fsl	official
22.	rsl	racial	40.	sˢ	sentence
23.	(whom)	whom	41.	Eˢ	chance
24.	dcvy	discovery	42.	jō	joy
25.	fsˢ'	efficiency	43.	—sy	mystery
26.	esl	essential	44.	ss	assistance
27.	u	understand	45.	lōˢ	allowance
28.	ˇdˢˢ	audiences	46.	ptl	potential
29.	nf—y	infirmary	47.	cdl	credential
30.	rōl''	royalties	48.	ony	honorary

Lesson Review

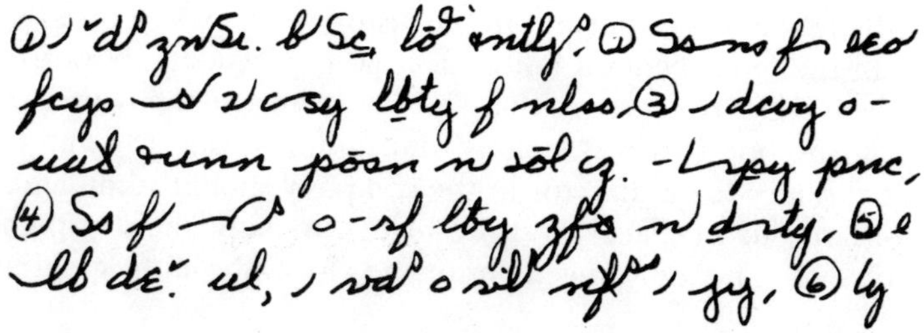

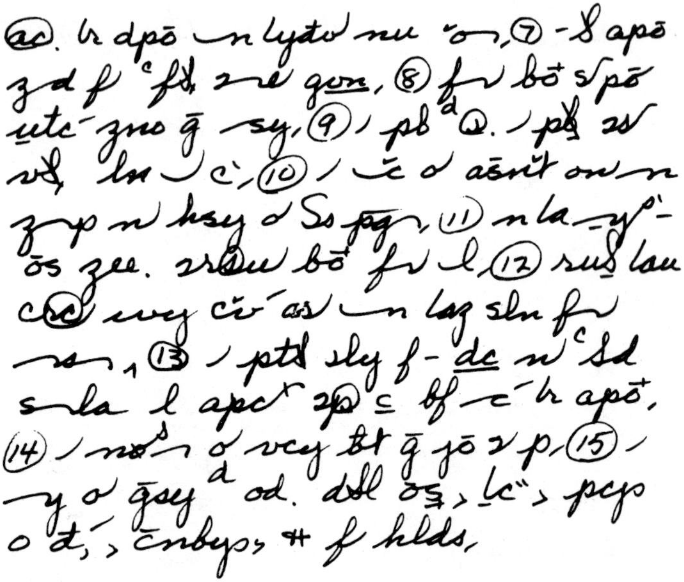

1. The audience was inspired by the speaker's loyalty and intelligence. 2. Specimens from each of the factories were sent to the chemistry laboratory for analysis. 3. The discovery of an unusual and unknown poison in the soil caused a temporary panic. 4. Space for the maintenance of a reference library was found in the dormitory. 5. He will be discharged unless the evidence of violence influences the jury. 6. They acknowledged their disappointment when they drove the new automobile. 7. A special appointment was made for the company officials to meet the governor. 8. From the boy's standpoint the undertaking was no great mystery. 9. The publicity department asked the publisher to send visuals along with the copy. 10. The walk of the astronaut on the moon was important in the history of the space program. 11. In that emergency a hoist was used to rescue the boys from the well. 12. Are you sure that you can recognize the ivory carving as the one that was stolen from the museum? 13. The potential salary for a director in the company should stimulate all applicants to prepare carefully before making their appointments. 14. The announcement of the victory brought great joy

to the people. 15. The manager of the grocery department ordered additional oysters, turkeys, packages of dressing, cranberries, etc., for the holidays.

Practice Guidelines for Lesson XII

Sounds

1. Avoid a long swing to the right:  not  .
2. Plural: tick the slash.
3. Remember that *y* is not written under  :  .
4. Plural: tick the bar: toys  . As noted, *oy* is treated like *ow* in that *h* is omitted before this symbol; and *nd, nt, n, d,* and *t* are omitted after it: hoist , point  .

With this lesson you have completed Sounds!

Vocabulary

9. If you pronounced this correctly, you wrote it correctly.

38. or .

Speed Building: Lessons I–XII

Be sure that you are seated comfortably so that you can relax and control your penmanship.

50 wpm = 24 seconds to each slash
60 wpm = 20 seconds to each slash
70 wpm = 17 seconds to each slash

Speed Drill

1. I am sorry that you have had so much delay in receiving the shipment of silk cloth that you wanted on May/ 20. The manager of the shipping room notified me that this cloth left our building on May 21, and/ the shipment was taken over by United Mail Service. I am inclined to believe that the cloth is/ being held in some freight yard in Chicago. Monday I sent a copy of your letter to the shipping department and today I/ received notice that they started a tracer on Tuesday. I am sure that we shall have something to report tomorrow./
2. Now that every wage earner can have an individual retirement account with tax shelters, Happy Valley/ Savings and Loan offers you a bonus for opening yours today. Just make the minimum deposit. At the/ end of the first period, we will send you a check for the money earned. Or if you choose we will deposit/ the earnings to your account. We promise to pay the highest rate for the full term of your deposit, and your account/ is insured to $100,000. If you deposit $1000 or more, we'll give you a special/ award: it's a full package of free banking services. So get a running start and make your first deposit today./

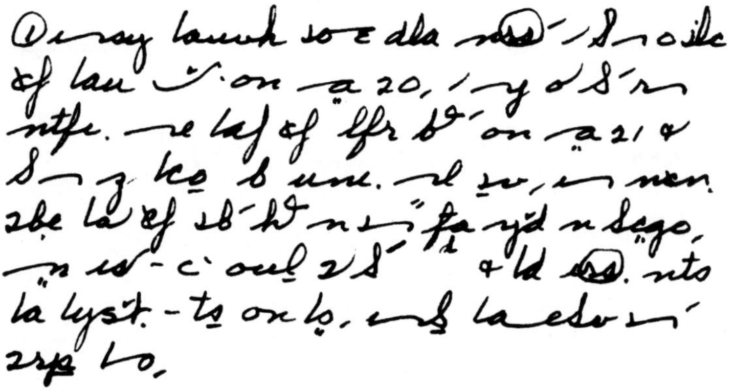

(2) nxlaeo y en co-r stencx-lx
D+ hp vl sv+ dlon of u-bns f opn-
u ld, fs-c-n dpst, a r o fs pd
-ls u-ec f-i en., o ifues
-eldpst / en+ sucx, -ep-s zpa
hs sa f fl L ou dpst ou cx snd.
2-HJD, ifudpst -nJD o o el
gv u-S a-d (:) ls-fl pyo fe bn-
ser, sogt-rn-st oc u fs dpst ld,

LESSON XIII

Prefixes and Suffixes

1. c = *com-*, *con-*, *cam-*, and *can-* when followed by a consonant.

campus cps	*comment c⌒	conceive csv
cancel csl	campaign cpn	compel cpl
comfort cft	*connote cno	candid cdd

*See Practice Guidelines

2. sp = *super-* The accent can be on either syllable.

supercede spsd	supersonic spsnc
superb spb	superficial spfs
superlative splv	superstition spst

3. ‿d = sound of *-werd*

onward on‿d	afterward af‿d	downward dn‿d

4. po = sound of *-poze*

impose ‿po	proposal p̄pol	indisposed ndpo.
repose rpo	compose cpo	disposal dpol

5. z = sounds of *-zy* and *-ize*

easy ez	compromise cp̄z	lazy lz
deputize dptz	crazy c̄z	revise rvz
busy bz	despise dSz	nosy nz

Memory Words

1.	lo	although
2.	lr	already
3.	nx	anxious
4.	cp	complete, completely, completion
5.	og	organize, organization
6.	mb	member
7.	f	finance, financial, financially
8.	c	country
9.	āg	agree, agreement, agreeable
10.	cd	condition
11.	dḡ	degree
12.	rmb	remember
13.	@	America, American
14.	dt	determine, determination
15.	sp	superintendent
16.	sf	certify, certificate
17.	aq	adequate, adequately
18.	av	advantage
19.	ō	employ, employment
20.	xp	explain, explanation
21.	spv	supervise, supervision, supervisory

Vocabulary

1.	bz	busy
2.	dpo	dispose
3.	cml	camel
4.	sfs	surface
5.	omd	homeward
6.	ōgn	overgrown
7.	nōz	noisy
8.	cd'	candy

9. overwork
10. cousin
11. torment
12. toward
13. repose
14. person
15. overdo
16. husband
17. lazy
18. anxious
19. uneasy
20. amply
21. wise
22. overall
23. concern
24. compare
25. thorough
26. country
27. comedy
28. wizard
29. onward
30. compute
31. consist
32. crazy
33. finance
34. worries
35. comply
36. civilize
37. store
38. awkward
39. western
40. expose
41. determination
42. remarkably
43. overcharge
44. suppose
45. surprise
46. consolation
47. department
48. recognize
49. composed
50. confidential
51. advantage
52. reliably
53. convention
54. backward
55. oversight
56. connive
57. commission

Phrase Drill

1.	xcsl	to cancel the
2.	idpo.	I am disposed
3.	xou	out of your
4.	@p	American people
5.	bfd	bring forward
6.	ngcd	in good condition
7.	ezsy	he was sorry
8.	lydd	they did not
9.	bfcvt	by this convention
10.	2lcsn.	to all concerned
11.	hsnvb	has never been
12.	pfd	please forward
13.	o x	with or without
14.	usspo.	you are supposed
15.	znsfi.	was not satisfied
16.	xduno	how do you know

Lesson Review

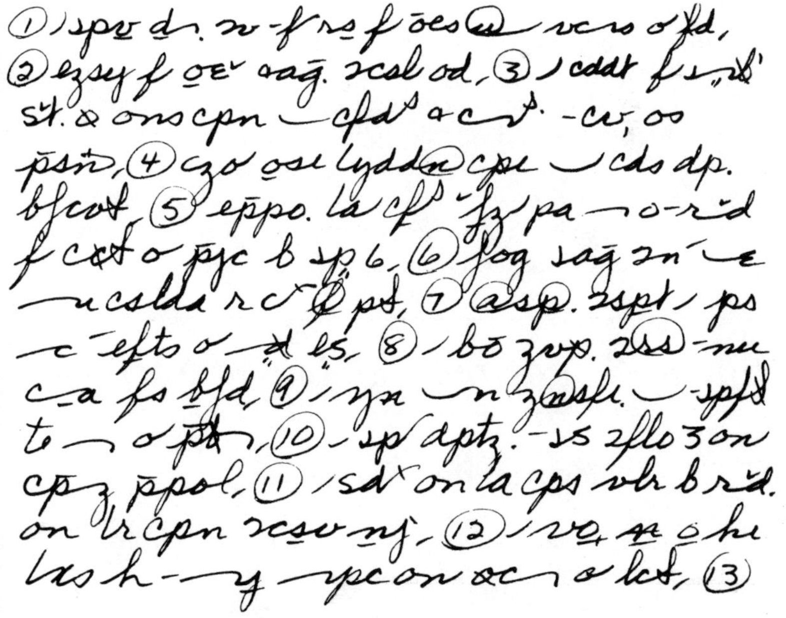

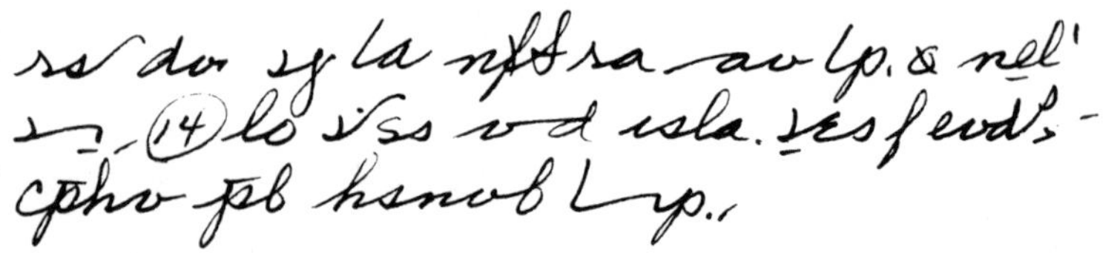

1. The supervisor determined to have a fund raiser for the employees who were victims of the flood. 2. He was sorry for the overcharge and agreed to cancel the order. 3. The candidate for the Assembly started out on his campaign with confidence and commenced a canvass of his precincts. 4. Because of the oversight they did not comply with the conditions adopted by this convention. 5. He proposed that the conference authorize the payment of a reward for the conclusion of the project by September 6. 6. This organization is agreeable to anything which might consolidate our country's financial position. 7. America is prepared to support the peace-making efforts of the Middle East. 8. The boy was very pleased to receive a new camera for his birthday. 9. The young woman was not satisfied with a superficial treatment of the problem. 10. The superintendent deputized an assistant to follow through on the compromise proposal. 11. The students on that campus have already been rewarded in their campaign to conserve energy. 12. The voters' anger over high taxes had a major impact on the outcome of the election. 13. Recent developments suggest that the inflation rate may have topped out in early summer. 14. Although scientists have made isolated searches for evidence, a comprehensive probe has never been attempted.

Practice Guidelines for Lesson XIII

Prefixes and Suffixes

1. Note how *comment* and *connote* are written: double consonants are usually treated as one; however when *m* or

n is doubled with these prefixes, write the duplicate consonant. Also write the *n* or *m* when vowels follow these prefixes: camera  , canoe .

Vocabulary

8. or .

12. *toward* does not have a *w* sound.

Lesson Review

4. If there could be any confusion between *adopt* and *adapt,* put the *a* in *adapt*; it is less frequently used than *adopt.*
5. Listen to *reward*: it follows the check sound rather than the *werd* suffix.

Some words are correctly pronounced more than one way, as in *candidate* in 3. Write what you hear.

LESSON XIV

Prefixes

1. D = *dest-*, *dist-*, *destr-*, *distr-*, *detr-*, and *deter-*. It may be underscored.

district Dc	destroy Dō	destination Dnt
distance Ds	distribute Dbu	deteriorate Da
disturb Db	destitute Dtu	detriment D—

2. C = *const-*, *constr-*, *conster-*, and *contr-*.

constrict Cc	contrary Cy	constitution Ct
contrast Cs	constant C'	consternation Cnt
contract Cc	control Cl	controversy Cvs'

3. R = *rest-*, *restr-*, and *retr-*.

restore Ro	restrain Rn	retract Rc
retreat Re	retrieve Rv	restricted Rc,
restaurant R'	retrogress Rg,	restitution Rt

Memory Words

1. cte committee
2. —' morning
3. s associate, association
4. ed educate, education, educational
5. n, nevertheless

6. communicate, communication
7. reasonable, reasonably
8. approximate, approximately
9. respond, response, responsible
10. additional, additionally
11. further
12. connect, connection
13. ordinary, ordinarily
14. circumstances
15. manufacture, manufacturer
16. return
17. increase, increasing, increasingly
18. arrange, arrangement
19. correct, correctly, correction
20. available, availability
21. necessary, necessity, necessarily
22. excellent

Phrasing Rule

Adjectives and adverbs are circled to indicate the phrase "as . . . as": as good as ; as fine as ; as near as ; as hot as ; as light as .

Memory Phrases

1. as much as
2. thank you, thank you for, thank you for your
3. thank you for your letter

4. as well as
5. please let
6. under separate cover
7. as soon as possible (this applies to any expression "as . . . as possible.")

Vocabulary

1. contraband
2. restrict
3. constitute
4. contralto
5. contest
6. retreat
7. distinct
8. construe
9. fault
10. contrive
11. restitution
12. responsible
13. disposition
14. retrocede
15. registration
16. educational
17. steward
18. restraint
19. disturb
20. edition
21. history
22. temperament
23. retribution
24. warrant
25. patience
26. destitute
27. consistent
28. missionary
29. contents
30. sorry
31. canvass
32. detest
33. services
34. ornamental
35. constituent
36. distinguish

37. destruction
38. constitution
39. encounter
40. punishment
41. contradict
42. detector
43. detract
44. retain
45. distant
46. detrimental
47. composition
48. intensify

Phrase Drill

1. as long as
2. in connection with
3. please let me go
4. if you will certify
5. it was difficult
6. as great as
7. can you remember
8. to help us
9. he was concerned
10. thank you for the
11. as sure as possible
12. as much as you can
13. just as well as not
14. to experience the
15. thank you for your letter
16. as near as I can judge

Lesson Review

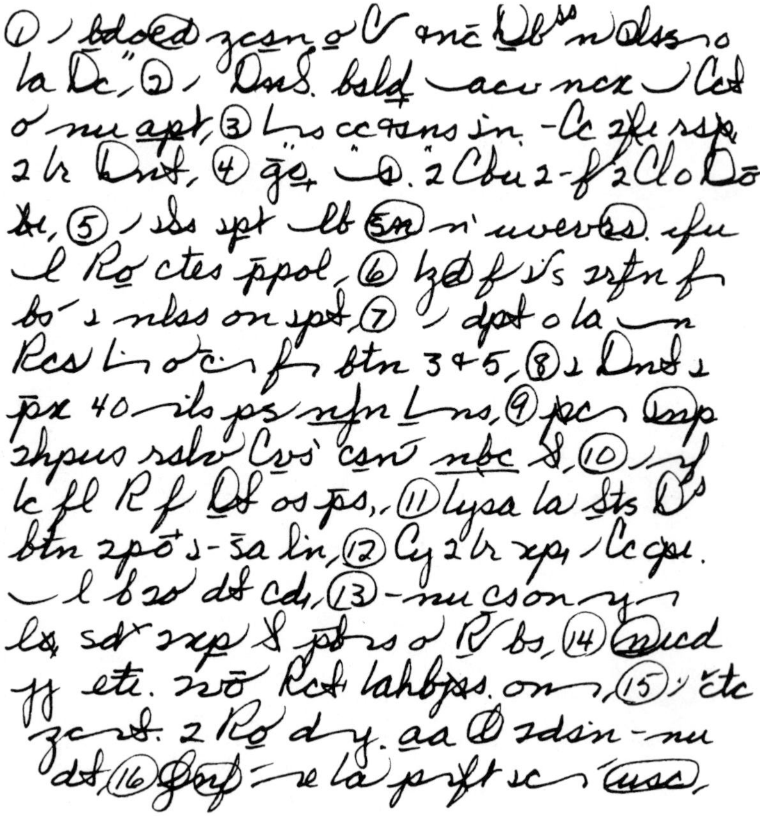

1. The Board of Education was concerned over the constant and increasing disturbances in the school system of that district. 2. The distinguished business leaders were active in connection with the construction of the new airport. 3. Thomas Cook and Sons signed a contract to fly our supplies to their destination. 4. Growers were asked to contribute to a fund to control or destroy the blight. 5. The association's support will be as strong as any you have ever received if you will restore the committee's proposal. 6. It was difficult for the scientist to refrain from basing his analysis on supposition. 7. The deposition of that woman

restricts the time of the crime from between three and five. 8. His destination is approximately forty miles past the northern terminus. 9. Please come as soon as possible to help us resolve the controversy concerning the NBC special. 10. The manufacturer took full responsibility for the deterioration of his process. 11. They say that the shortest distance between two points is a straight line. 12. Contrary to their expectations the contract complied with all but two of the additional conditions. 13. A new course on management allows students to experience the special problems of the restaurant business. 14. As near as I could judge he tried to void the restrictions that had been placed on him. 15. The architect was commissioned to restore the damaged area as well as to design a new addition. 16. Thank you for informing me that the pamphlet is coming under separate cover.

Practice Guidelines for Lesson XIV

3. *rest-* may be underscored.

Phrasing Rule

Note how end of circle stroke may be used to score or to cross a *t*.

Phrase Drill

1. The circle stroke continues to make the bar of and in 6 it becomes an overscore.

Lesson Review

1. One capitalization signal can apply to an entire name if it is phrased together.

LESSON XV

Prefixes and Suffixes

1. N = *entr-*, *intr-*, *enter-*, *inter-*, *inst-*, and *instr-*.

entry	N'	introduce	Nds	entertain	Ntn
interest	Ns	instant	Nt	instruct	Nc
interval	Nvl	instrument	N⌒	intercede	Nsd

2. E = *electr-*.

electron	En	electrode	Ed	electrician	Eʃ

3. P = *para-* and *parti-*.

parallel	Pll	participate	Ppa	parable	Pb
partisan	Psn	paraphrase	Pfs	particle	Pc
parasite	Psi	participle	Psp	paragon	Pgn

4. p = sound of *per-* in words of two or more syllables.

perform	pf⌒	purpose	ppo	perceive	psv
purple	pp	personnel	psnl	pursue	psu
pertain	ptn	permission	p⌒ʃ	perfunctory	pfny

5. G = *graph* as a prefix or suffix.

paragraph	PG	graphite	Gi	graphic	Gc
photographer	ftG	biography	bG`	lithograph	lfG

6. ⓢ = *-stic*.

domestic	dⓢ	artistic	ʻtⓢ	enthusiastic	nfⓢ

Memory Words

1. congratulate, congratulations
2. particular, particularly
3. statistics, statistical
4. beyond
5. often
6. even, evening
7. enter, entrance
8.* o'clock
9. prompt, promptly
10. investigate, investigation
11. merchandise
12. permanent
13. electric, electrical, electricity
14. establish, establishment
15. immediate, immediately
16. certain, certainly
17. another
18. practice, practical, practically
19. universe, universal
20. continue, continuous, continuously, continuation
21. demonstrate, demonstration

*See Practice Guidelines

Vocabulary

1. implement
2. interfere
3. drastic
4. sensual

5. itself
6. already
7. bacteria
8. parachute
9. telegraph
10. theories
11. farther
12. paradise
13. intent
14. courage
15. plastic
16. majestic
17. elastic
18. oyster
19. graphite
20 persuade
21. members
22. poultry
23 cancellation
24. connection
25. biographic
26. instrument
27. yourself
28. partition
29. confident
30. committee
31. rustic
32. permanent
33. purple
34. interview
35. particle
36. period
37. perfect
38. given
39. partisan
40. mileage
41. permit
42. growl
43. sensible
44. graphic
45. mystic
46. purse
47. electrocute
48. merchandise
49. autobiography
50. geographer
51. pursue
52. entrance
53. paradox
54. myself
55. interrupted
56. optimistic

57. sarcastic
58. comparative
59. participant
60. entertain
61. electrotype

62. disturb
63. engage
64. perception
65. perjury
66. guard

Phrase Drill

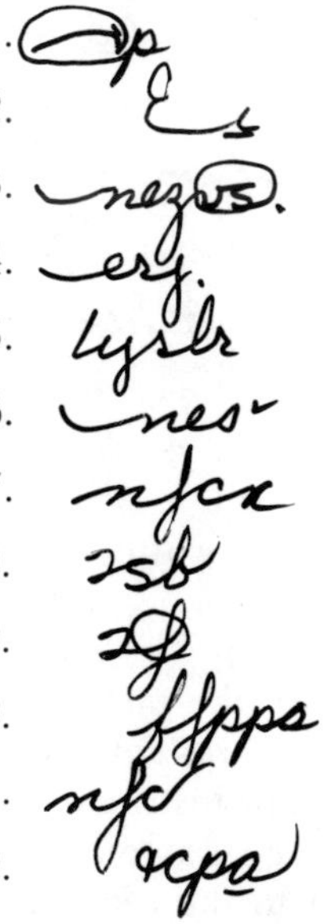

1. as many as possible
2. electric wire
3. when he was investigated
4. we arranged
5. they are already
6. when he saw
7. in this connection
8. to establish the
9. to thank you for
10. for this purpose
11. in this country
12. and compare the

Lesson Review

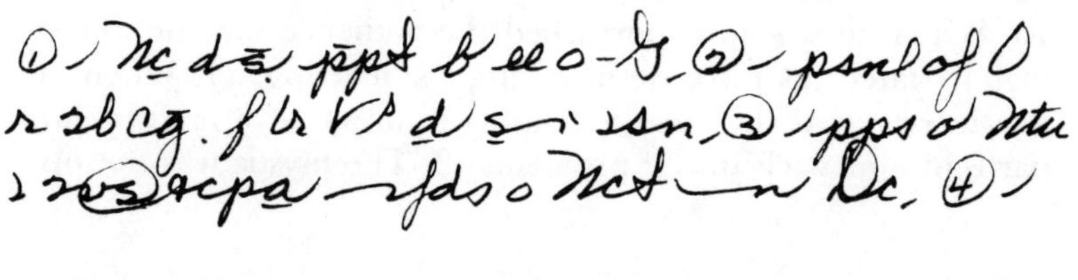

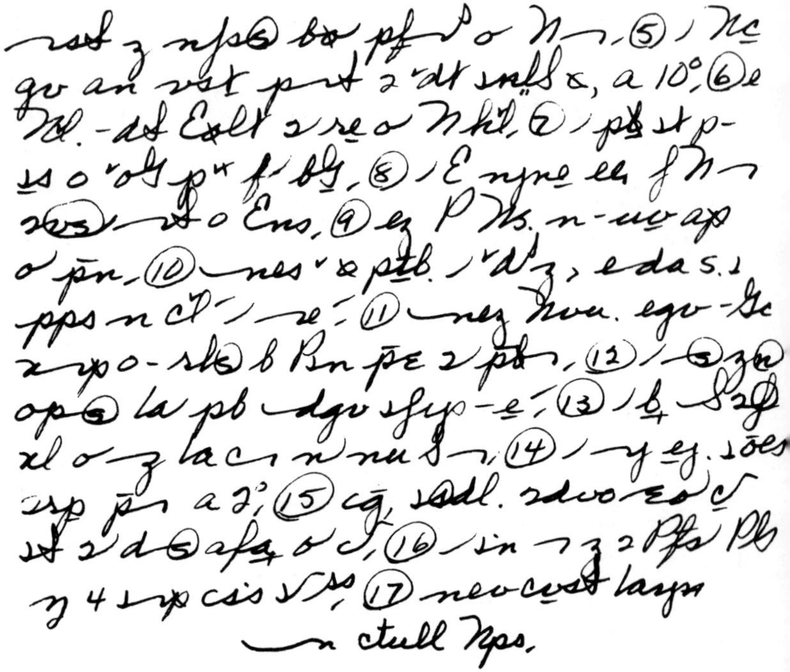

1. The instructor demonstrated the proposition by the use of a graph. 2. The personnel of this office are to be congratulated for their attendance during the stormy season. 3. The purpose of the institute is to investigate and compare the methods of instruction within the district. 4. The musician was enthusiastic about the performance of the instrument. 5. The instructor gave another visitor permission to audit his English class at ten o'clock. 6. He installed an additional electric outlet to the rear of the entrance hall. 7. The publisher set up a series of autograph parties for the biographer. 8. The electrical engineer uses this instrument to investigate the motion of electrons. 9. He was particularly interested in a universal application of the principle. 10. When he saw how perturbed the audience was, he immediately stated his purpose in calling the meeting. 11. When he was interviewed, he gave a graphic example of a realistic but partisan approach to the problem. 12. The mystic was not op-

timistic that the public would give his theories a hearing. 13. The buyers wish to thank you for the excellence of the merchandise that came in the new shipment. 14. The manager urged his employees to report promptly at two o'clock. 15. Congress is scheduled to devote much of the current session to the domestic affairs of the country. 16. The assignment was to paraphrase the paragraph into four simple, concise sentences. 17. In every conversation, that young woman continually interrupts.

Practice Guidelines for Lesson XV

Prefixes and Suffixes

4 is used only as a prefix: comparable cpb. One syllable words: perch pe, purge pj, purse ps.

5 may be used alone as a Memory Word. As a suffix it may be underscored.

Memory Words

8. More about time: 5 p.m. 5p; 6:30 a.m. 6 30 a.

Vocabulary

36. Listen! This word does not have the *per* sound. How would you write *perish*? p8 !

LESSON XVI

Prefixes and Suffixes

1. T = *trans-*.

transfer Tf transplant Tpv transaction Tacf
transit Tt transmission Tmf transistors Tss

2. X = *extr-* and *exter-*.

extreme Xm exterminate Xmna extradite Xdi
exterior X extravagant Xvg external Xnl

3. ª above the writing line equals the single syllable prefix *ab*.

abstract ªsc abstain ªsn abnormal ªnml
absent ªv absurd ªsd abscond ªQv

4. ° above the writing line equals the single syllable prefix *ob* and the suffix sound of *us*.

jealous jl° serious s° observe °sv
obligation °lgf famous fm° generous jn°
obtain °tn object °jc obstinate °snt

5. / = sounds of *-ety, -ity,* and *-sity*. It is called *ity*.

activity acv/ simplicity smpl/ city s/
society ss/ curiosity c/ propriety ppp/
capacity cp/ dignity dgn/ locality lcl/

6. b/ = *-bility*.

liability lb/
capability cpb/
flexibility fxb/
stability sb/
desirability dsrb/
inability inb/

Memory Words

1. entitle
2. hard
3. perhaps
4. balance
5. invest, investment
6. salesman
7. cooperate, cooperation, cooperative
8. represent, representative, representation
9. transport, transportation
10. national
11. administration, administrative
12. otherwise
13. commerce, commercial
14. express, expression
15. absolute, absolutely
16. children
17. specify, specific, specifically, specification
18. correspondence, corresponding

Vocabulary

1. music
2. abduct
3. cooperate
4. absolve
5. rustic
6. obscure

7. interfere
8. absurd
9. external
10. available
11. abscond
12. translate
13. extreme
14. potential
15. contradict
16. sagacious
17. courageous
18. sarcastic
19. transform
20. obstinate
21. transport
22. capabilities
23. extricate
24. simplicity
25. ferocity
26. valorous
27. locality
28. serious
29. royalty
30. transact
31. quantity
32. boundary
33. transfer
34. distress
35. obvious
36. charity
37. posture
38. brevity
39. superior
40. sagacity
41. society
42. obedient
43. handful
44. rescue
45. abuse
46. oblong
47. dangerous
48. inability
49. corresponding
50. extraneous
51. extradition
52. possibility
53. absolutely
54. probability
55. extravagant
56. cautiously

57. obligation
58. sensitive
59. endurance
60. injuries
61. transparent
62. abdomen
63. transgress
64. various
65. responds
66. visibility

Phrase Drill

1. to conclude the
2. he will notice the
3. must be settled
4. can be made
5. please let us use
6. that has the
7. to my credit
8. of your city
9. few months ago
10. you represent the
11. in so far as
12. on her part
13. at your suggestion
14. in his efforts
15. cooperate with us

Lesson Review

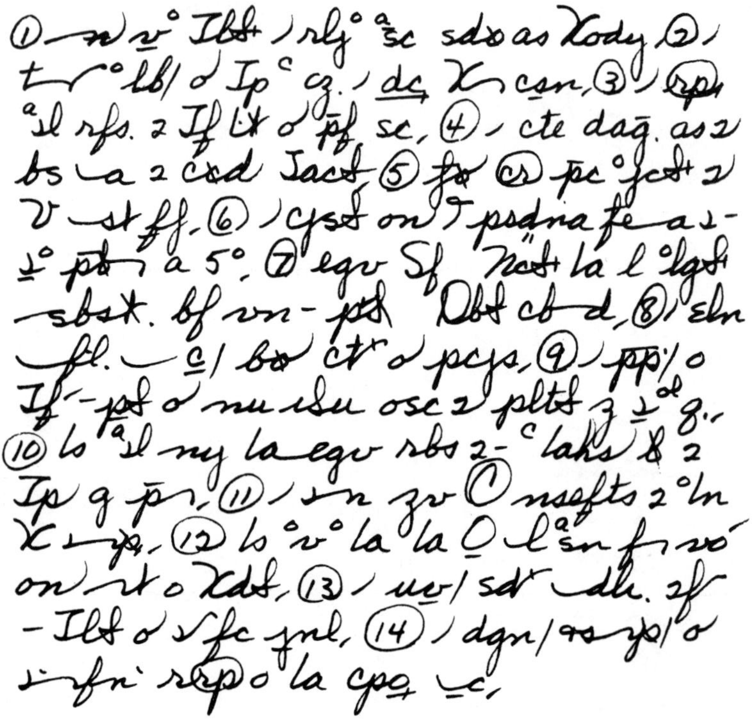

1. Among the various translations, the religious abstract stood out as extraordinary. 2. The tremendous liability of the transportation company caused the directors extreme concern. 3. The representatives absolutely refused to transfer title of the preferred stock. 4. The committee disagreed as to the best way to conclude the transaction. 5. Throughout the correspondence practical objections to the investment were set forth. 6. The congestion on the old Pasadena Freeway is a serious problem at five o'clock. 7. He gave specific instructions that all obligations must be settled before even a partial distribution can be made. 8. The children were filled with curiosity about the contents of the packages. 9. The propriety of transferring a portion of the new issue of stock to the politician was seriously questioned.

10. It is absolutely necessary that we give our business to a company that has the ability to transport the goods promptly. 11. The salesman was very cooperative in his efforts to obtain extra samples. 12. It is obvious that that officer will abstain from voting on the matter of extradition. 13. The university students were delighted to find a translation of the scientific journal. 14. The dignity and simplicity of the symphony are representative of that composer's work.

Practice Guidelines for Lesson XVI

Prefixes and Suffixes

2. *Extr* should be written without a pen-lift:  ; not  or . It may be underscored. Alone it is the Memory Word *extra.*
3. *ab* that is not a single syllable: abolish 
4. *ob* that is not a single syllable: oblige 
5. The *ity* stroke starts above the writing line at about the height of an ordinary letter, and slants down to the left until it breaks the writing line. The word *city* requires the writing of the *s* sound. Plural: double the stroke: cities 

Vocabulary

48. The dot just before the *n* distinguishes this word from *nobility.*
56. Note how the *ly* suffix is reduced in size and joined to the *ous*: 

Speed Building: Lessons I–XVI

50 wpm = 24 seconds to each slash
60 wpm = 20 seconds to each slash
70 wpm = 17 seconds to each slash

Speed Drill

This letter will introduce Miss Mary Randall whom we are sending to you to fill your temporary secretarial/ position as you requested. Miss Randall has been a member of our staff of temporary employees/ for five years. She has been thoroughly tested for her stenographic ability and she knows our policy on/ office ethics and cooperation. Although she will be working in your location, she is actually an/ employee of ours. You will find this to be desirable since it eliminates all your payroll details/ and expenses. At the end of the week, or on completion of the assignment, she will show you a time card specifying/ the hours she spent on the job. After you approve this record, she will mail it to us. We will then pay her/ and bill you for the service. Please let us know if you have any questions. Thank you for using our agency./

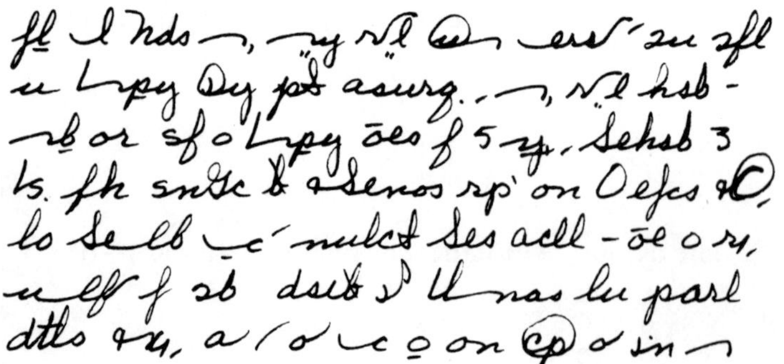

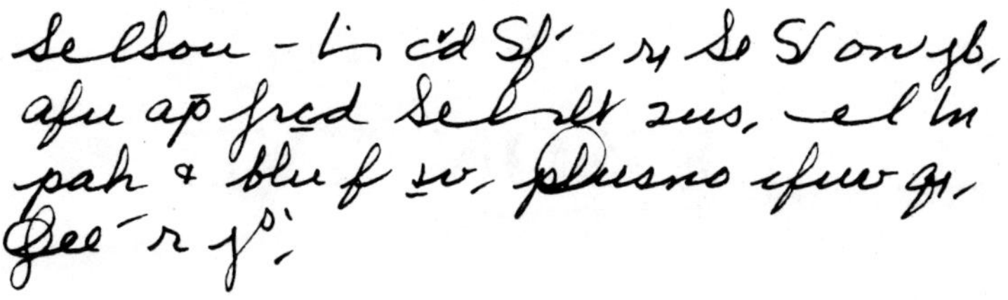

LESSON XVII

Suffixes

1. ċ = *-tic.*

mathematics mfċs pathetic pfċ political plċ

2. l above the writing line = *-ingly.*

smilingly sml^l lovingly lv^l jokingly jc^l

3. l below and through the writing line = *-edly.*

supposedly spo_l dejectedly djc_l decidedly dsd_l

4. n above the writing line = sounds of *iun* and *yun.* It is called *yun.*

reunion run^n onion n^n companion cpn^n
criterion ctr^n oblivion °lv^n aliens al^ns

5. f = *-ification.*

classification clsf notifications ntfs
identification df

Memory Words

1. cp accomplish, accomplishment
2. ⁄s industry, industrial
3. js adjustment
4. ns insure, insurance
5. id idea, ideal
6. bu· beauty, beautiful

7. © corporate, corporation
8. ad advertise, advertisement
9. rc recommend, recommendation
10. % per cent, percentage
11. gl guarantee, guaranty
12. ^c indicate, indication
13. t true, truly, truth
14. (s) sincere, sincerely
15. cd according, accordance, accordingly
16. (s) respect, respectfully
17. (v) invoice
18. 1s first
19. 2d second

Phrasing Rule

Whereas a circle around a word indicates "as . . . as," a half circle or arc above the word indicates the phrase "more . . . than" and an arc below the word indicates the phrase "less . . . than."

more acceptable than	ax	less acceptable than	ax
more agreeable than	ag	less eager than	eg

These symbols can also indicate "more than" and "less than":

less than expected	xp.	more than 5%	5%
more than enough	nf	less than two	2

Vocabulary

1. s^l seemingly
2. b^s balance
3. dic dramatic
4. cd accordance
5. al^n alien
6. fgic phlegmatic

7. decidedly
8. companion
9. emphasize
10. democratic
11. literature
12. repeatedly
13. circularize
14. laughingly
15. oblivion
16. Canadian
17. transmit
18. appreciate
19. bookkeeper
20. authentic
21. possibly
22. industries
23. nullification
24. association
25. critic
26. drown
27. asthma
28. dominion
29. promise
30. quartz
31. another
32. glorious
33. opinion
34. guardian
35. refer
36. champion
37. baptize
38. oldest
39. million
40. emphatic
41. athletic
42. degree
43. lumber
44. luncheon
45. willingly
46. extricate
47. energetic
48. rejoice
49. undoubtedly
50. notification
51. questionable
52. feasibility
53. merchandise
54. sparingly
55. communicate
56. arithmetic
57. mortification
58. union

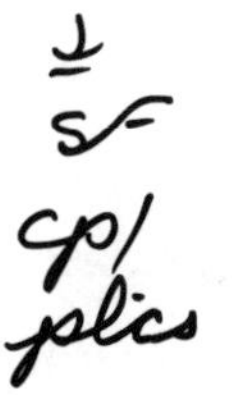
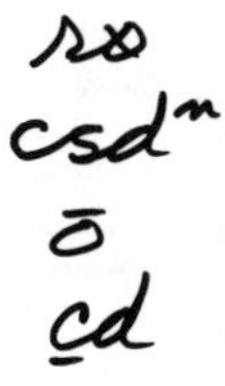

59. certain
60. standard
61. capacity
62. politics
63. around
64. custodian
65. employment
66. accordingly

Phrase Drill

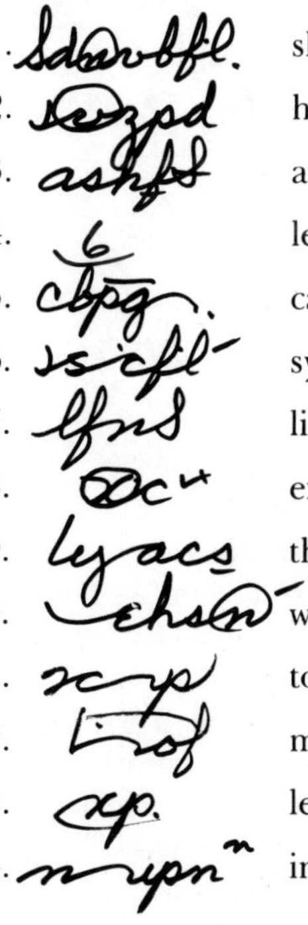

1. should not have been filed
2. his invoice was paid
3. as her fortune
4. less than six
5. can be programmed
6. systematic filing
7. life insurance
8. express cars
9. they may consider
10. which has nothing
11. to accomplish the
12. more time off than
13. less than expected
14. in my opinion

Lesson Review

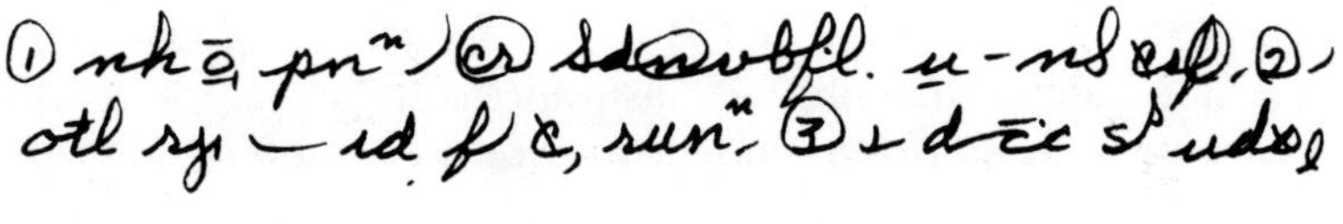

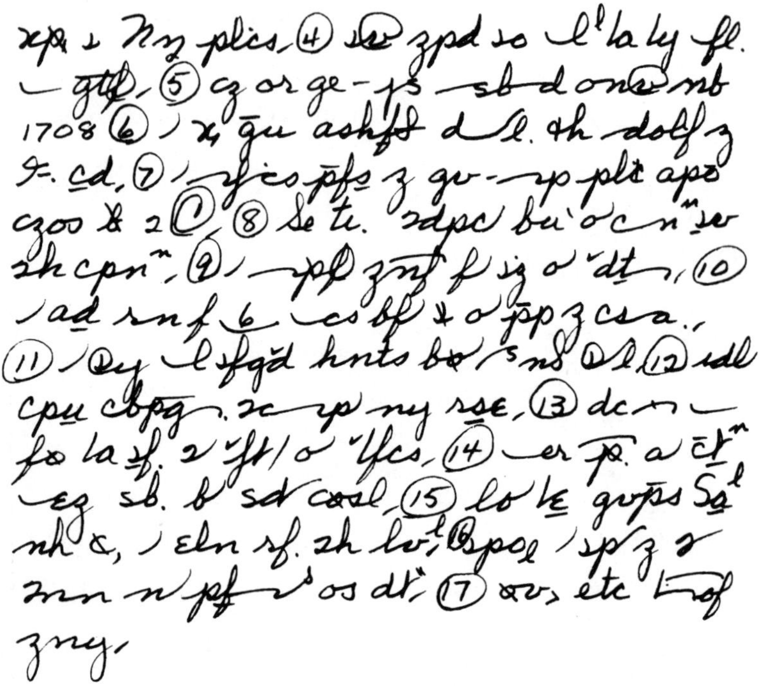

1. In her employer's opinion the correspondence should not have been filed under an insurance classification. 2. The hotel arrangements were ideal for the class reunion. 3. His democratic stance undoubtedly explains his entrance into politics. 4. His invoice was paid so willingly that they were filled with gratification. 5. Because of our guarantee an adjustment must be made on invoice #1708. 6. The expenses grew as her fortune dwindled and her mode of life was altered accordingly. 7. The mathematics professor was given an important political appointment because of his ability to cooperate. 8. She tried to depict the beauty of the communion service to her companion. 9. The amplification was more than enough for the size of the auditorium. 10. The advertising ran for less than six weeks before the sale of the property was consummated. 11. The secretary will safeguard her notes about the industrial insurance scandal. 12. Ideally the computer can be programmed to accomplish the necessary re-

search. 13. Documents were found that certified to the authenticity of the artifacts. 14. We are more than pleased at the criterion which was established by the student council. 15. Although the teacher gave praise sparingly in her class, the children referred to her lovingly. 16. Supposedly the superintendent was second to none in the performance of his duties. 17. However, he took more time off than was necessary.

Practice Guidelines for Lesson XVII

Suffixes

1. The *tic* goes under  : automatic . It can be slashed. Be sure that *tic* is a word ending: for example, *tic* cannot be used with *identical*  (or  , although the former is preferred because it is shorter) or *article* . Plural: add *s*.
2. *ingly* is in the position of *ing*.
3. *edly* is in the position of *suffix*.
4. Plural: join small *s* to *yun*.
5. Plural: add *s*.

Memory Words

2 and 12. Join small *s* to make plural.

18. This is the numeral "1" + *small, disjoined* Cooper *s*.
19. This is "2" + *ent*. Other ordinal numerals are formed the same way: 3d, 4f, etc.

LESSON XVIII

Prefixes and Suffixes

1.  = *centr-* and *center-*.

centerboard  centralize  centrifugal 

2.  = the negative true prefixes *il* before words beginning in *l; im* before words beginning in *m*; and *ir* before words beginning in *r*.

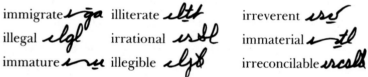

immigrate  illiterate  irreverent 
illegal  irrational 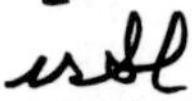 immaterial 
immature  illegible  irreconcilable 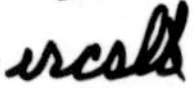

3.  = the single syllable prefixes *ad-* and *at.*

admire  atom  admission 
Atlantic 

4.  above the writing line equals the prefix *sub* and the suffix *ness.*

submarine  fondness 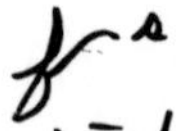 subsidy 
happiness 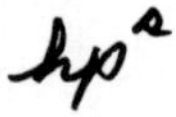 sacredness  subordinate 

5.  = *-tude.*

attitude  multitude 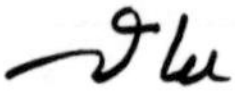 aptitude 

Memory Words Based on Longhand Abbreviations

 = accom. = accommodate, accommodation

 = aver. = average

 = benef. = benefit, beneficial

 = cap. = capital, capitol

 = cat. = catalog

 = con. = convenience, convenient, conveniently

 = deliv. = deliver, delivery

 = dup. = duplicate

 = exam. = examine, examination

 = fed. = federal

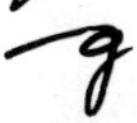 = mag. = magazine

 = mem. = memorandum

 = misc. = miscellaneous

 = oppor. = opportunity

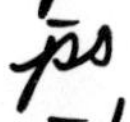 = pres. = president, present, presently

 = prod. = produce, production, productive, productivity

 = R.R. = railroad

 = re. = regard, regarding, regardless

 = remit. = remittance

 = sub. = subject

Vocabulary

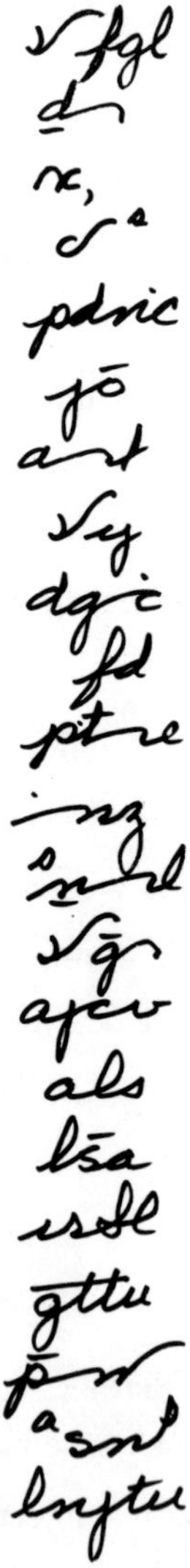

1.	absurdity	23.	centrifugal
2.	idleness	24.	determination
3.	telegraph	25.	excess
4.	immature	26.	kindness
5.	adjacent	27.	pedantic
6.	excitedly	28.	adjoin
7.	impatient	29.	admit
8.	immaterial	30.	century
9.	Corinthian	31.	dogmatic
10.	irrevocable	32.	federal
11.	disagreement	33.	epitome
12.	adjustments	34.	immunize
13.	stenographer	35.	subnormal
14.	irretrievable	36.	centigram
15.	substantial	37.	adjective
16.	sensitiveness	38.	atlas
17.	irrefutable	39.	illustrate
18.	immeasurable	40.	irrational
19.	consciousness	41.	gratitude
20.	centerpiece	42.	prominent
21.	centralize	43.	abstinence
22.	immediately	44.	longitude

45.	cc	Arctic	56.	op	opportunity
46.	avs	advance	57.	ajr	adjourned
47.	sdu	subdue	58.	smt	submit
48.	amrb	admirably	59.	sntl	central
49.	sstu	substitute	60.	aj	adage
50.	xdl	exceedingly	61.	mpls	impulse
51.	strn	subterranean	62.	ahe	adhere
52.	ndts	indebtedness	63.	aptu	aptitude
53.	snbl	sensibility	64.	fts	fitness
54.	amsfe	atmosphere	65.	avct	advocate
55.	ilta	illiterate	66.	epg	epigram

Phrase Drill

1. colda were consolidated
2. aucn at your convenience
3. evcs every consideration
4. reo regardless of the
5. urp you are prepared
6. nfc in this country
7. fsefts for his efforts
8. sft were sufficient
9. 5 more than five
10. lcbsd it can be studied

11. that he had been
12. please remember
13. thank you for your consideration
14. foreign exchange
15. if you are sure

Lesson Review

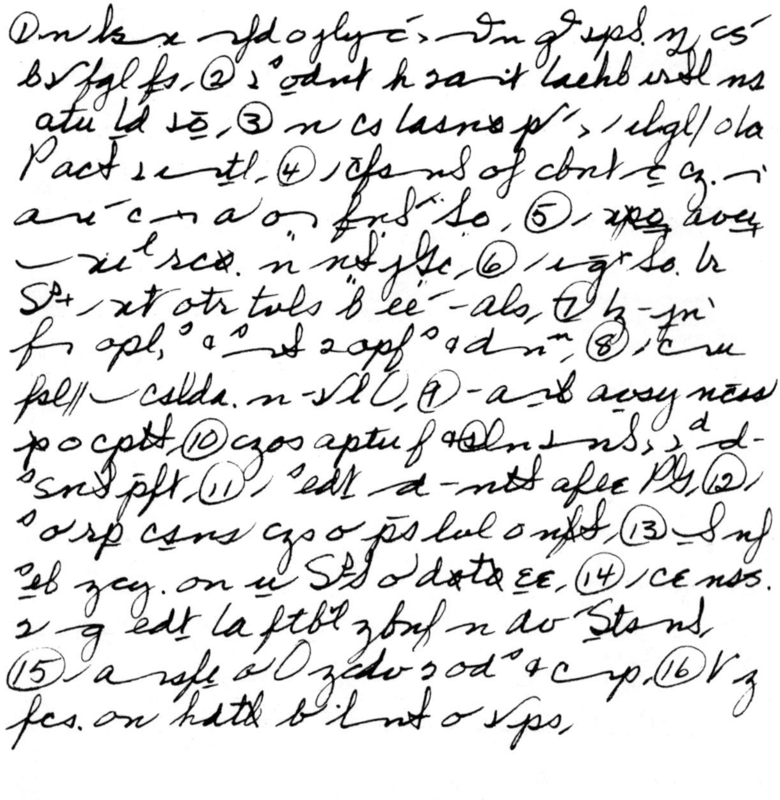

1. In the lost wax method of jewelry making, molten gold is pushed into the casting by centrifugal force. 2. His subordinate had to admit that he had been irrational in his attitude toward his employer. 3. In the case that is now pending, the illegality of that particular action is immaterial. 4. The craftsmanship of this cabinet maker caused many admiring comments at the Home Furnishings Show. 5. The explorers' adventures were excitingly recounted in *National Geographic.* 6. The immigrants showed their sponsors the extent of their travels by using an atlas. 7. It was a journey from hopelessness and submission to hopefulness and dominion. 8. The community facilities were consolidated in a central office. 9. An admirable adversary increases the pleasure of competition. 10. Because of his aptitude for and skill in salesmanship, his department made a substantial profit. 11. The subeditor made a notation after each paragraph. 12. The subject of the report concerns the causes of the present level of inflation. 13. Worship in this suburb was carried on under the sponsorship of the downtown church. 14. The coach insisted to the magazine editor that football was beneficial in developing sportsmanship. 15. The atmosphere of the office was conducive to orderliness and accomplishment. 16. Attention was focused on the head table by the illumination of the centerpiece.

Practice Guidelines for Lesson XVIII

Prefixes and Suffixes

1. As with all symbols that end above the line within a word, the following part of the word is written close to the first part of it.

   He seldom sold him anything. 

   He sent Peggy a centerpiece. 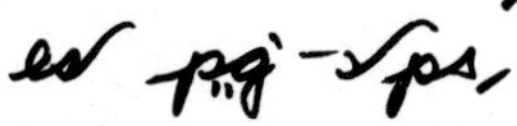

2. Examples of words beginning with *ill, imm,* and *inn* where this rule does *not* apply:

illustrate ĺsa immense  innate ˋna

3. Example of *ad* that is not a single syllable: adult dt; example of *at* that is not a single syllable: atone ln.
4. Use a small complete *s* above the line rather than initial *s*. Position it close to the rest of the word.

Memory Words

"Production" is more frequently used than *product.* Since they could be confused, write *product* according to theory: p̆dc.

This is the final group of Memory Words given in this text. However you are encouraged to make your own to fit the special vocabulary of your business or study.

Vocabulary

In 5, 28, and 57, the *d* of *ad* is not pronounced: listen, don't visualize!

In 7 the root word does not start with *m*: therefore the negative prefix *im* cannot be used.

Note how the two small suffixes are joined in 19.

LESSON XIX

Suffixes

1. = *-logy.*

genealogy apology biology

geology

2. = *-logical.*

pathological zoological chronological

3. = *-scribe.*

conscribe describe inscribe

transcribe

4. = *-scription.*

subscription description conscription

States

The following abbreviations are those approved by the United States Postal Department:

Alabama AL

Alaska AK

Arizona AZ

Arkansas AR

California CA
Colorado CO
Connecticut CT
Delaware DE
Florida FL
Georgia GA
Hawaii HI
Idaho ID
Illinois IL
Indiana IN
Iowa IA
Kansas KS
Kentucky KY
Louisiana LA
Maine ME
Maryland MD
Massachusetts MA
Michigan MI
Minnesota MN
Mississippi MS
Missouri MO
Montana MT
Nebraska NE
Nevada NV
New Hampshire NH
New Jersey NJ
New Mexico NM
New York NY
North Carolina NC
North Dakota ND
Ohio OH
Oklahoma OK
Oregon OR
Pennsylvania PA
Rhode Island RI
South Carolina SC
South Dakota SD
Tennessee TN
Texas TX
Utah UT
Vermont VT
Virginia VA
Washington WA
West Virginia WV
Wisconsin WI
Wyoming WY
District of Columbia DC

Vocabulary

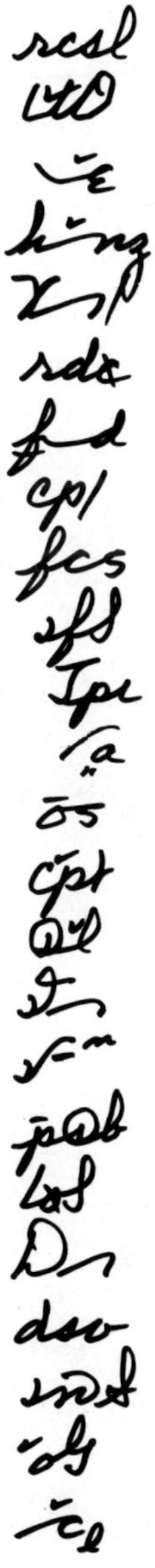

1. smilingly
2. biological
3. pliability
4. superscription
5. retrospect
6. graphology
7. delightful
8. enthusiasm
9. futuristic
10. antiseptic
11. preliminary
12. magnitude
13. consensus
14. introduced
15. constrictive
16. irretrievable
17. destructible
18. disposition
19. heaviness
20. overwhelm
21. Peruvian
22. contingency
23. boisterous
24. casually
25. reconcile
26. tautology
27. watch
28. harmonize
29. extremity
30. radical
31. forward
32. capacity
33. forecast
34. selfish
35. transpire
36. India
37. hoist
38. carpet
39. squall
40. seldom
41. centurion
42. prescribe
43. township
44. detriment
45. decisive
46. sanction
47. autograph
48. markedly

49. Atlantic
50. reposing
51. welder
52. creation
53. deftness
54. electrify
55. particle
56. prowess
57. contrast
58. immature
59. parallel
60. odious
61. abscond
62. hope
63. unsung
64. shawl
65. subsist
66. obvious
67. glisten
68. adamant
69. central
70. entrance

Phrase Drill

1. I will be able
2. one of our
3. thank you for the
4. as much as I'd like
5. we would appreciate your
6. more credit than
7. we would like
8. in my possession
9. and I will expect
10. of great importance
11. as far as I know
12. did you mention

13. on this occasion
14. his knowledge of
15. I must ask you
16. at this point
17. if you think
18. you might ask
19. every day
20. it was considered
21. if it is convenient
22. each of the
23. if possible
24. we regard
25. you have nothing
26. nothing else
27. there isn't

Lesson Review

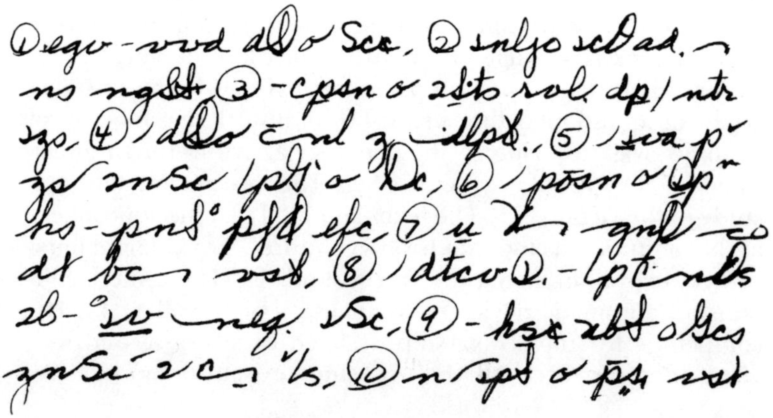

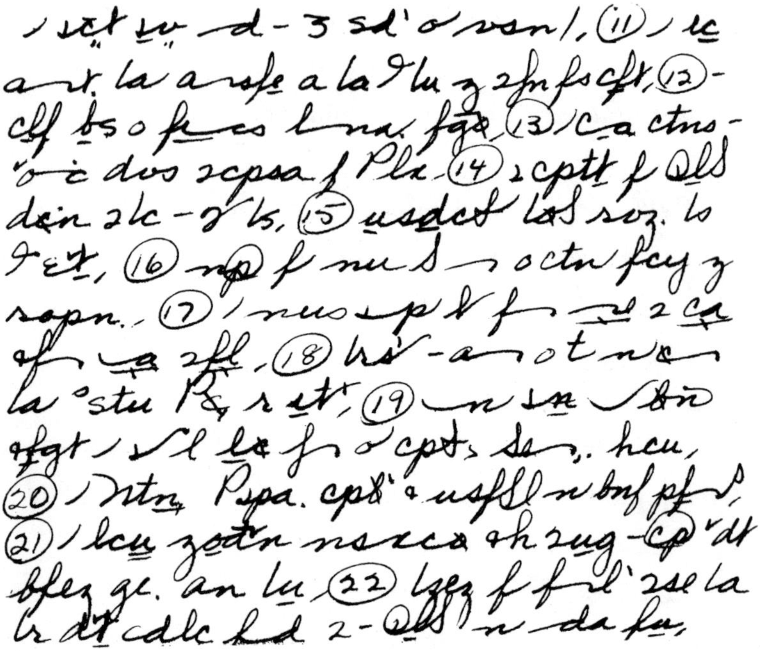

1. He gave a vivid description of the spectacle. 2. His knowledge of psychology aided him in his negotiations. 3. A comparison of the two shirts revealed the disparity in their sizes. 4. The description of the criminal was widely published. 5. The survey party was sent to inspect the topography of the district. 6. The poison of the scorpion has a pernicious pathological effect. 7. Under extreme magnification the microdot became visible. 8. The detective asked a top criminologist to be an observer when he questioned the suspect. 9. A historical exhibition of graphics was inspiring to the commercial artist. 10. In anticipation of the President's visit, the Secret Service made a thorough study of the vicinity. 11. The hiker admitted that the atmosphere at that altitude was too thin for his comfort. 12. A colorful burst of fireworks illuminated the foreground. 13. The camera contains an automatic device to compensate for parallax. 14. His competitor for the scholarship declined to take a second test. 15. Under his direction the township revised its old charter.

16. In preparation for the new shipment of cotton, the factory was reopened. 17. The news swept the land from Maine to California and from Washington to Florida. 18. There isn't an atom of truth in the claim that the substitute particles are irritants. 19. When the singer went blank and forgot the central lyrical theme of the composition, she missed her cue. 20. The entertainers participated capably and unselfishly in the benefit performance. 21. The lecturer was overdrawn in his expense account and had to undergo a complete audit before he was guaranteed another tour. 22. It was easy for the family to see that their daughter could look forward to a scholarship in the immediate future.

Practice Guidelines for Lesson XIX

Suffixes

1. Plural: use the tick: apologies 
2. Use  for the Memory Word *logical.*

States

Remember that the longhand *k* is used in initials.

Vocabulary

10 and 36. It is not usual to start a word with *ent*; however some words, particularly those that start with *ant,* can be written and read quickly by doing so: antagonist , antecedent , anticipate , antidote . In such words, be sure the disjoined part is close under the *ent.*

Lesson Review

8. Note *criminologist*: 

The vocabulary list and the sentences in this lesson cover almost all of the sounds, theories, prefixes, and suffixes of Quickscript.

LESSON XX
BUSINESS CORRESPONDENCE

A correct address is necessary not only to facilitate the delivery of a letter but also as a matter of courtesy. The address at the beginning of a letter is called the superscription.

The following abbreviations may be used only for the designated purposes.

Superscription Abbreviations

1.	p	Place	11.	s	South
2.	b	Building	12.	w	West
3.	Q	Square	13.	s	Street
4.	bl	Boulevard	14.	nc	Incorporated
5.	w	Way	15.	c/	Care of
6.	pc	Park	16.	eQ	Esquire
7.	d	Drive	17.	eQ.	Esq.
8.	r	Road	18.	nc.	Inc.
9.	n	North	19.	a	Avenue
10.	e	East			

If your letter calls for an attention line, use the Memory Word for *attention.* Type it two spaces below the superscription either centered or at the left margin. Use no punctuation after it.

Salutation Abbreviations

1. Dear Mr.
2. Dear Mrs.
3. Dear Miss
4. Dear Ms.
5. Dear Dr.
6. Dear Sir
7. Dear Madam
8. Messrs.
9. Mesdames
10. Gentlemen

If the letter calls for a subject line, use the Memory Word for *subject* and follow with a colon. If you use *Re* or *In Re,* write or without punctuation. The subject line is always typed two spaces below the salutation and is either centered or even with the left margin.

Complimentary Close Abbreviations

1. Yours truly
2. Very truly yours
3. Yours very truly
4. Cordially
5. Cordially yours
6. Respectfully yours
7. Yours respectfully
8. Sincerely
9. Sincerely yours
10. Yours sincerely

Write city names as they sound or use their popular abbreviations. Note that city names always have the capitalization symbol under them; state names use the capitalized initials symbol:

Los Angeles Louisiana

You will develop quick ways of writing city names that you use frequently. Now that you have the full system of shorthand, what works for you is what is right for you: the criteria are speed in writing and ease in reading.

City names may never be abbreviated when you transcribe them. Names of states may be abbreviated, but preferred practice is to write them in full.

Practice Letters

1. Mr. Donald Burton
5216 Tracy Street
Tuscon, Arizona 85707

Dear Mr. Burton:

Thank you for your order of June seventh. As you instructed, it was sent by express on June fifteenth and insured for $200.00.

If we can serve you further, we shall be glad to do so.

Yours truly,

2. Fashion Center, Inc.
123 Seventh Avenue
Buffalo, New York 14206

Gentlemen:

In Re Invoice #1903

Thank you for your corrected bill for the month of December. I understand that the error was caused by a similarity in the names of the accounts: hereafter I shall charge to Robert Grant Brown rather than to R. G. Brown.

The promptness with which you rectified this matter is indeed appreciated. I am enclosing my check for $284.56, the amount due.

Very truly yours,

3. Mr. Arthur Amestoy, President
Georgetown Iron Works
Akron, Ohio 44321

Dear Mr. Amestoy:

This letter will introduce to you Mr. Henry Brooks who is visiting your factory with the idea of gathering material for a survey of industrial relations.

It would be very much to his advantage if he could meet you personally in order to learn your opinions in several areas connected with this report.

I shall appreciate whatever assistance you give him.

Sincerely yours,

4. Dr. Martin Cass
10 Columbia Building
Des Moines, Iowa 50321

Dear Dr. Cass:

Through Mr. Ernest Campbell we have just learned of your generous contribution to the support of the Compton Crisis Center. It is a pleasure to acknowledge your gift and to tell you that you have done something that is of great value.

For some time there has been a great need for an additional counselor. Your gift will make this possible. Literally hundreds of desperate men, women, and young people will be indebted to you in the coming year. They will not be able to thank you. On their behalf, I do so now.

Cordially yours,

5. Roosevelt Plaza Hotel
   Pershing Square
   Boston, Massachusetts 02136

   Attention Mr. Klein

   Gentlemen:

   Please reserve for Mrs. Burdick and me a room with twin beds and bath from April seventh through April fifteenth. We appreciated the quiet room on the back of the building, sixth floor, that we were given when we last visited.

   Our plane does not arrive until 6:30 p.m. We should be able to check in by 7:30.

   Yours very truly,

6. Ms. Diana Russell
   10 Edgemont Road
   Madison, Wisconsin 53710

   Dear Ms. Russell:

   This is to confirm my telephone conversation with you on September 8, 1979, in regard to the second mortgage which you want to have placed on your house located at 2001 North Hoover Drive, Indianapolis.

   The terms agreed upon are as follows: a secured note of

$10,000 with interest at 10% per annum, principal and interest payable in monthly installments of $212.50 for sixty months.

Will you please call at this office as soon as possible so that our attorney can prepare the necessary documents and procure a preliminary title report.

Very truly yours,

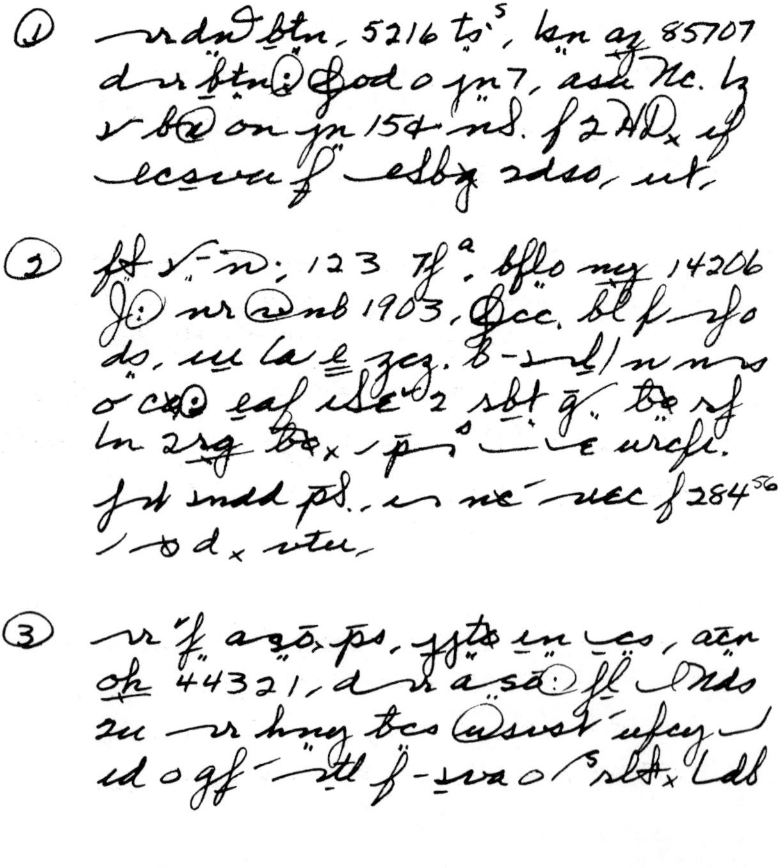

[illegible]

(4) [illegible]

(5) [illegible]

(6) [illegible]

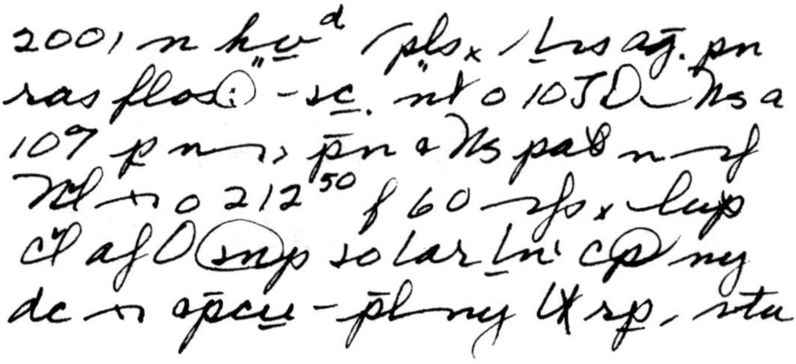

LESSON XXI
SPEED BUILDING

If you have been practicing the Speed Drills at the end of every four lessons, you should be able to take dictation now at 60 words per minute. This lesson is meant to push you to higher speeds.

It starts with five groups of sentences based on word-use frequency. Start with the first group of sentences and, as in the previous Speed Building sections, drill on each sentence individually by dictating to yourself. Increase your speed until you are writing as fast as you can. Make yourself relax. Keep your penmanship controlled. Can you read your notes easily? Have you been accurate? Drill with the words you have hesitated over or written incorrectly.

At this point work with a friend or tape recorder by having the sentences you've been practicing dictated consecutively. Ignore the sentence numbers: they are not counted. Start at 50 or 60 wpm. Don't scrawl! Relax!

Words per minute	Dictation time for every 20 words
50	30 seconds
60	20 seconds
70	17 seconds
80	15 seconds
90	13 seconds
100	12 seconds

Each group of 20 words is indicated by a slash.

Drill the same way with the other groups of sentences.

Repeat this process and increase your speed by 10 wpm until

you are writing 80 wpm. This will not happen overnight! Daily practice builds speed.

The shorthand for the following five groups of sentences is provided at the end of this lesson. In the practice letters which follow the sentences, the accuracy of your transcription will be the test.

Sentences Based on the 300 Most Frequently Used Words

1. Please use the information which is enclosed in this letter.
2. I can appreciate that it was their interest/ that made the program work.
3. They ordered many copies to be sent to our department also.
4. It is now possible/ to make company policy.
5. We like your office more each year.
6. One of these days I will know who is new in/ the business.
7. He should thank each one who has been here for two years.
8. There are so many who are up and about only/ because of our service.
9. Were you with them during that time?
10. Some of us have gone all out to help others do as well/. (100 words)

Sentences Based on the 600 Most Frequently Used Words

1. It is necessary to complete the accounts before the special meeting.
2. Some of the people are not/ interested in the school area at present.

3. I may send in my insurance check within the next three days.
4. Let me/ first state how good it is to find that an additional opportunity is available.
5. However, I/ wish to plan for the future course of action after I see what the people want and need.
6. You wish to give the matter/ further consideration.
7. The report, due in the city every month, has not been received.
8. The sales cost is/ up another percent.
9. That is the same form that was used last time.
10. Every request is numbered and returned by mail/. (120 words)

Sentences Based on the 900 Most Frequently Used Words

1. Now that we have paid off the loan in full, our home is truly our own.
2. He sent his application to the Federal/ Building.
3. It is important that you attach invoices for personal property.
4. Copies of the contract/ with the hospital were sent to the attention of the Supply Department of National Products Association/.
5. I will advise that the bill for several tax periods will increase unless receipts can be found.
6. The/ employees are happy in their jobs.
7. Please credit the following payment for equipment to the new public high school/.
8. I am enclosing the basis for the recent set-back in prices.
9. If you can provide a better system, members/ of the board will be very pleased.
10. Are you in a position to offer the general committee free books out of stock/? (140 words)

Sentences Based on the 1200 Most Frequently Used Words

1. Why question the records of that shipment?
2. The representative will serve in the field until the delivery/ plans become effective.
3. The manager is glad that we were able to pay the charges on all the items this/ past week.
4. The management of government services is an issue concerning the President.
5. The bank requested/ facts in addition to the current required statements.
6. If problems continue, we will know there is no/ cooperation between the educational system and the community.
7. The customer probably cannot/ show the value of group savings.
8. The college recruits staff from various organizations.
9. The county claims the/ right to purchase power and water from another state.
10. They will change the annual rates if production is too small./ (140 words)

Sentences Based on the 1500 Most Frequently Used Words

1. I suggest that dealers get together immediately for an end-of-the-year sale in every store.
2. He needs/ training in writing advertising.
3. The planning agency is working to meet family needs.
4. This type of/ community development needs individual support in order to get the benefits and protection/ of good administration.
5. He took the old-looking law books home to study.
6. There will be little control in the/ district unless they schedule an inquiry on the original question.

7. High quality merchandise is/ always appreciated.
8. In defense of that industry, it has never once given evidence of lack of trust./
9. Put the cover on the box and you will notice the fine construction.
10. In consideration of the benefits/ of weeks of regular care, it gives me pleasure to make a direct cash payment covering the completed project./ (160 words)

Now go on to the practice letters.

Practice Letters

If you achieved 80 wpm with the sentences, start at 60 wpm with the letters. No superscriptions are given in these letters because addresses are not included in speed tests—accuracy in recording names and addresses is more important than speed. However, the salutation and complimentary close are included in the word count.

Work with the letters as you did with the sentences, increasing your speed as you develop your skill. Keep your writing controlled and compact.

#1
Dear Mrs. Brown:

Although your name was placed on our list of charge customers some time ago, we have no record of/ your ever having used your account.

Are we in any way at fault?

We'd appreciate a frank reply and we/ enclose a stamped envelope for your convenience.

We hope the enclosed announcement of the new Spring fashions will tempt you to visit us.

Sincerely yours, (66 words)

#2
Gentlemen:

Thank you for your concern over my unused charge account. I am not comfortable in waiting on/ myself. I prefer to have the attention, help, and even advice of a courteous, caring salesperson. As/ a result I do most of my shopping in stores that provide that service.

Would it be possible to provide two/ levels of service? Keep things just as they are for those who prefer it, but also provide a few trained personnel/ to assist people who are willing to pay a small extra fee for personalized attention for those of us who/ are confused by the do-it-yourself system.

This would be much appreciated.

Very truly yours, (118 words)

#3
Dear Dick,

Before calling a special meeting of the company employees, the reports of several important/ management committees need to be considered.

Will you please schedule a working session as soon as possible/ for the members of the Executive Board? It would be wise to invite representatives of the concerned committees to join us. Miss Henderson will be glad to give you their names.

Please emphasize the urgency of a full attendance.

Yours, (84 words)

#4
Dear Sir:

Thank you for your check which covers your telephoned order of January sixth.

Our shipping department/ informs me that the first half of the order has already been sent. However the second carton, containing/ the shelving sections, will be delayed until some of the shelves are refinished: several pieces had small scratches/ on them, and we are unable to reorder a new supply.

We are sorry the complete order could not be sent/ at the same time.

Very truly yours, (86 words)

#5

Dear Miss Jackson:

I enclose the original and one copy of a proposed Partnership Agreement for your/ new venture. Since you are not sure just how your plans will develop, I have made the Agreement as generalized/ as possible.

After your partner has reviewed the Agreement, please call or write me if she has any comments, changes,/ or suggested improvements. As you will see, when the names and values are inserted, the Agreement will be/ in condition to be signed if you both find it satisfactory.

Yours truly, (94 words)

#6

Dear Senator Jones:

I have learned of the possibility that a filibuster may be attempted to prevent/ the Senate from voting on SB 123. Such an effort, if successful, would deprive our citizens/ of their right to a considered exercise of legislative judgment in this matter, and benefit only/ those senators who lack the courage to expose their feelings to their constituents.

I do not know what your own/ opinion may be on the merits of this bill. However, I urge you, as a matter of conscience, to use your/ influence to discourage a filibuster so that this important issue may be fairly heard and decided.

Respectfully, (123 words)

#7

Dear Friends:

I am happy to announce the opening of my own salon, His and Her Hair Fashions, at 900/ South Main Road.

As a former member of Andy's staff, I wish to extend my heartfelt thanks for your past patronage./ However, because this venture is a fresh start for me, I shall welcome any support which you can provide.

Drop in/ for a cup of coffee and meet Carla, a specialist in hair tinting, and Mr. Bob, well known for his feather/ cutting techniques. Also you will meet Josie, our expert manicurist. I shall continue as the hair stylist./

Rest assured that we will not fail your expectations. You will be receiving the most attentive service available./

Please call for an appointment at 765-4321.

Cordially, (135 words)

#8

Gentlemen:

The Community Improvement Association requests that members of the Planning Commission/ give serious consideration to the development of the public property between Ellis Avenue/ and Grove Street in the 3800 block.

Our district has no park within its boundaries. Indeed the closest/ recreational development is across the freeway and therefore unavailable to pedestrians. Increased/ home construction has reduced open-lot playgrounds and has caused more families to move into the area.

At/ present the property is of no use to anyone, and we are told the city has no plans for it.

Members/ of our Association will be glad to meet with you either downtown or here in our district.

Yours very truly, (140 words)

Several businesses were cooperative in giving information about their shorthand testing procedures for secretarial applicants. A few offices accept 60 wpm for 'light' shorthand, but 80 wpm is the general minimum. In some offices tapes are used to dictate to applicants, and in others the tests are given personally. A major television studio uses Short Tapes, which are standardized, copyrighted dictation materials for testing from 60 to 110 wpm.

The following letters are some that have been used to test applicants. They vary as to how they count words, and each letter is prefaced by the actual instructions used.

#1
80 Words Per Minute
Dictation Time: 1 minute

Dear Sir:

Many people in our city get double use from their checking accounts. To begin with, they use it as a practical and logical way to pay their bills. Then, they use it as a family budget. The checkbook records all the money deposited and paid out so that from day to day the family knows how much it has to work with.

If you do not have a checking account with our bank, by all means open one today.

Yours truly,

#2
90 Words Per Minute
Dictation Time: 1 minute

Dear Mr. Taylor:

In an effort to eliminate wasted seats that travel empty when some people make reservations, purchase tickets, and then do not show up at departure time, we decided a few days ago to institute the following policy effective June 1:

Service charge equal to 25% of the fare will be made when passengers fail to use or turn in their tickets prior to the departure of the plane.

It is our belief that this policy will make it possible for our patrons to secure seats when they want them.

Very cordially yours,

#3

Scoring: The following letter dictated within 90 seconds equals 80 wpm; within 75 seconds, 90 wpm; within 60 seconds, 100 wpm; within 40 seconds, 120 wpm.

Gentlemen:

Thank you for your check for $57.95 in payment of our invoice dated October 1st, from which you have deducted the 2% cash discount.

Of course, you know we allow a cash discount as a premium for prompt payment to be deducted only when payment is made within 10 days from the date of the invoice.

So we are enclosing your check as we think you would much prefer to have the account settled in full rather than to have it show a small balance.

Will you write out a check for $59.10 and mail it in at once?

Yours very truly,

With the above letter, there was also a list of 47 words with instructions to the applicant to check those incorrectly spelled.

#4

The following letter is one from Short Tapes, a dictation speed-building cassette system, used by some organizations to test applicants. This particular letter is dictated at either 60, 70, or 80 wpm.

For the same speeds, follow instructions on p. 137, 138.

Dear Customer:

As a special thank you to the present customers of our data center and a means of/ introducing our service to prospective customers, we are making a special limited offer. For/ every reel of computer tape you store with us, you may purchase directly from us a brand-new 2000-foot/ reel of tape as listed above.

Dayton, Incorporated, maintains in each of our centers high security,/ climate-controlled vaults for off-site protection of vital computer tapes. Messenger service, reference,/ retrieval, re-filing, and up-to-date exchange programs are all available.

This is a limited offer./ Prices are subject to change.

For more information call 348-2207.

Sincerely,/

#5

Dictate: 80 wpm in 3 minutes, 100 wpm in 2½ minutes, 120 wpm in 2 minutes.

/ = 80 wpm // = 100 wpm /// = 120 wpm

Dear Miss Jones:

We are delighted that you have decided to work for Thomas Temporaries.

We can assure you that you will find your new career extremely interesting, pleasant, and above all profitable. Profitable both in income and experience. You will broaden your knowledge in many areas as you learn the ways of American business in many different industries. You will find yourself in new places, with assignments/ taking you to insurance companies, banks, legal firms, advertising agencies, TV and radio stations, and on occasion// to the door of some famous celebrity. All will be fun and rewarding, and you will have the personal satisfaction/// of making a real contribution.

Thomas Temporaries is your employer. We are not an employment agency. We assign you and we pay you. You pay no fee for this service. You will receive a good hourly wage, less the legally/ required deductions such as Social Security, federal withholding, and state disability insurance//.

Our staff is dedicated to serving you. Our greatest desire is that you are pleased. We want your association/// with us to be a lasting one. We hope you will be so pleased that you will refer your friends to us, as the need for Thomas Temporaries is growing rapidly.

Again, welcome to your company and your new friends.

Sincerely,

Shorthand for Sentence Groups

300 Most Frequently Used Words

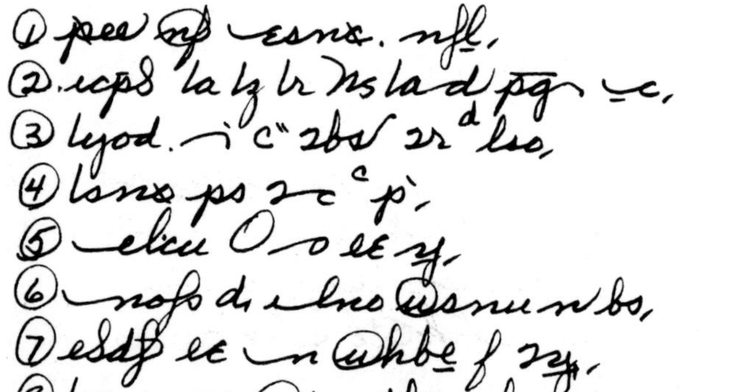

600 Most Frequently Used Words

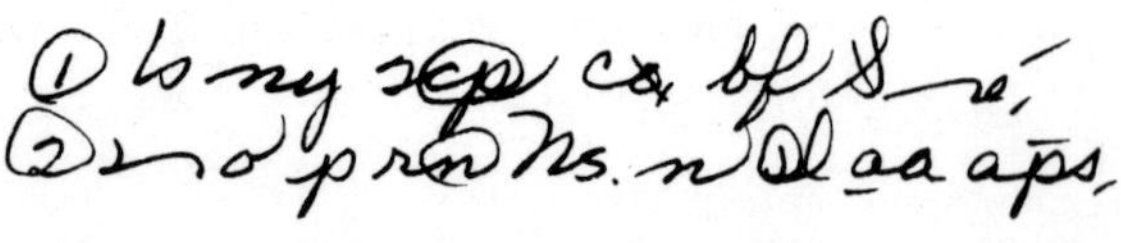

(3) sa vn u nsec in nx 3 ds,
(4) lt se is s og b sf la-dt op svl,
(5) ovi 8 spnf fuc soact afise
p and,
(6) u 8 sgv st f cs,
(7) rp, dn sl ev f, hs bss.,
(8) cs sp an 7,
(9) las f lazee. ls,
(10) ev rq snb. st. bl,

900 Most Frequently Used Words

(1) nt la eopd of lon nfl, ro, tron,
(2) es sap f fd b,
(3) ls p lau atc f ps pp,
(4) c o Cc hstl o sp o
nt pdcs s,
(5) lis la bl f sw lx pds lncs ul,
rses cbfx,
(6) ōes r hp n lr gbs,
(7) p flo pa f gp nupb hul,
(8) nc bss f rs t bc n pss,
(9) ifucpsvd - bt s, o bd lb sp.,
(10) sun pt sf pr cte fe bcs oosc,

1200 Most Frequently Used Words

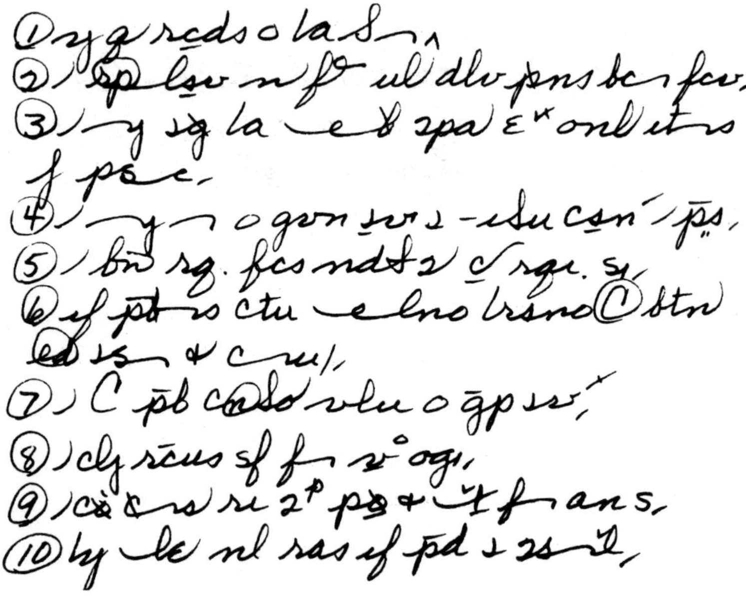

1500 Most Frequently Used Words

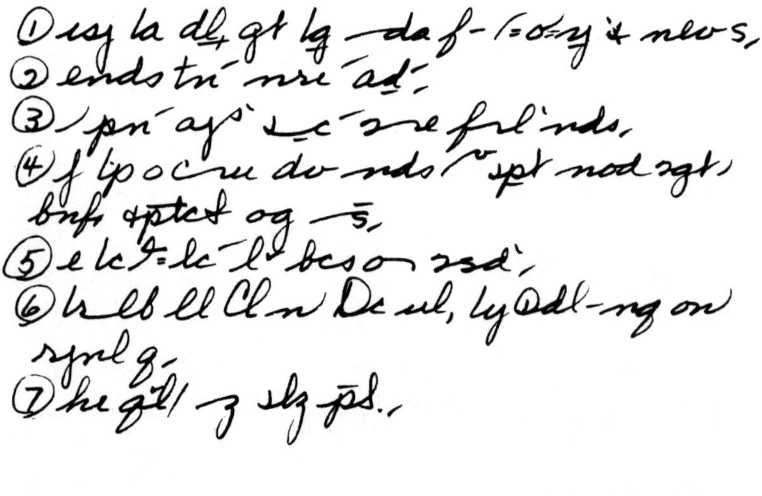

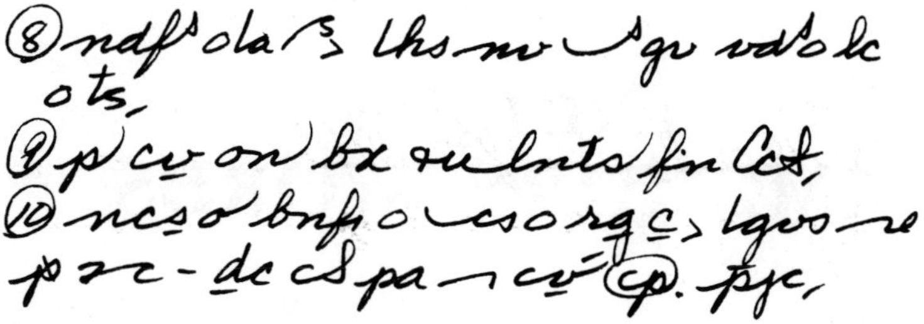

INDEX OF MEMORY WORDS

- a, an
- ability
- able
- absolute, absolutely
- accept, acceptance, acceptable
- accommodate, accommodation
- accompany
- accomplish, accomplishment
- accordance, according, accordingly
- acknowledge, acknowledgment
- additional, additionally
- adequate, adequately
- adjustment
- administration, administrative
- advance, advancement
- advantage
- advertise, advertisement
- advice, advise, advisable, advisory
- after, afternoon
- again, against
- age
- ago
- agree, agreement, agreeable
- all

already
although
always
am
America, American
and
another
answer
anxious
anything
appear, appearance, apparent, apparently
apply, application, applicable
appointment
appreciate, appreciation, appreciative
approve, approval
approximate, approximately
April
are
arrange, arrangement
ask
assistance, assistant
associate, association
assure, assurance
at
attention
August
auto
automobile
available, availability
average
balance
be, been
beauty, beautiful
because
before
behind
belief, believe
benefit, beneficial

correspondence, corresponding
country
credit
customer
day, daily
December
definite, definitely, definition
degree
deliver, delivery
demonstrate, demonstration
department, departure
determine, determination
develop, development
difficult, difficulty
disappointment
do
dollar
dozen
due
duplicate
during
educate, education, educational
electric, electrical, electricity
employ, employment
enclose, enclosure
end
enter, entrance
entitle
envelope
especially
establish, establishment
etc.
even, evening
ever, every
everything
examine, examination
excellent
except, exception, exceptional, exceptionally

expect
expense, expensive
experience
explain, explanation
express, expression
extra
favor, favorable, favorably
February
federal
finance, financial, financially
first
for
Friday
friend, friendly
from
further
general, generally
given
glad, gladly
go, good, goods
government, governmental
graph
great, greatly
guarantee, guaranty
had
hard
have
he
hear, here
heard
help, helpful
her
him
his
hour
however
hundred
idea, ideal
immediate, immediately
import, important, importance
in

include, inclusion, inclusive
increase, increasing, increasingly
indicate, indication
individual, individually
industry, industrial
inform, information
inquire, inquiry
insure, insurance
into
invest, investment
investigate, investigation
invoice
is
it
January
July
June
letter
little
logical
magazine
manage, manager
manufacture, manufacturer
many
March
market, marketing
matter
maximum
May
member
memorandum
men
merchandise
million
minimum
miscellaneous
Monday
money
month, monthly
more
morning

Mr.
Mrs.
national
nature, natural, naturally
near, nearly
necessary, necessarily, necessity
never
nevertheless
newspaper
nor
not
note
nothing
November
number
o'clock
October
of
office
often
old
only
opportunity
order, orderly
ordinary, ordinarily
organize, organization
other
otherwise
our
ourselves
over
paper
part, party
particular, particularly
people
per cent, percentage
perhaps
permanent
person, personal, personally
please, pleasant, pleasure
policy

position
possible, possibly, possibility
practice, practical, practically
prepare, preparation
present, presently
president
principal, principle
probable, probably, probability
produce, production, productive, productivity
prompt, promptly
proper, properly, property
public, publicity
publish, publication
purchase
put
question
railroad
really, realize
reasonable, reasonably
receive
reception
recognize, recognition
recommend, recommendation
refer, reference
regard, regarding, regardless
register, registration
regret
regular, regularly, regulation
remember
remittance
reply
report

represent, representative, representation
request
respect, respectfully
respond, response, responsible
return
sale
salesman
satisfaction
satisfactory, satisfactorily
satisfy
Saturday
second
secretary, secretarial
secure, security
self
separate, separately
September
service, servicing
several
shall
ship
sincere, sincerely
something
special, specially
specify, specific, specifically, specification
standard, standardization
state, statement
statistics, statistical
store
subject
succeed, success, successful, successfully
suggest, suggestion
Sunday
superintendent
supervise, supervisory, supervision
supply

sure, surely
taken
telephone
than
thank, thanks
that
the
them
themselves
then
there, their
they
thing
this
thorough, thoroughly
those
thousand
through
Thursday
to, too
today
together
tomorrow
transport, transportation
true, truly, truth
Tuesday
two
under, understand
understood
universe, universal
until
up
upon
use, useful
very
was
Wednesday
were
where
who
why
with
women
year, yearly
yesterday
you, your

Phrases

 as much as

 as well as

 as . . . as possible

 please let

 thank you, thank you for, thank you for your

 thank you for your letter

 under separate cover

Any use of Wright MacMahon Shorthand symbols and theory is made with the consent and approval of Margaret Wright MacMahon, the originator of that system.